The Psychology of Insider Threat Prevention

Part Two

Unifying Continuous Performance Management

&

ITP Cyber Security

Systems Management Institute, Orlando, Florida 32835.

This book is available at a special discount when ordered in bulk quantities. For more information, contact Publications Sales Department, SMI Press, Orlando, Florida 32835, Tel: (407) 864 7756

www.smirrsp.com

www.drraynewkirk.com[1]

1. http://www.drraynewkirk.com

Table of Contents

Preface.....1
Introduction to This Series.....4
The Formative Questions.....6
1: Our Memory, Our Life.....7
2: Newkirk Axiom.....22
3: Existential Hunger.....26
4: Level Two Existential Hunger.....40
5: Level Three Existential Hunger.....49
6: Spiritual Relationship.....52
7: Complex Relationships.....58
8: Rational Side of Relationships.....64
9: Designing Potent Relationships.....78
Description of Terms.....85
References & Historical Bibliography.....91
-A –.....93
-C-.....99
-E-.....103
-F-.....104
-G-.....105
-H-.....106
-I-.....107
-J-.....108
-K-.....109
-L-.....110
-M-.....112
-N-.....117
-O-.....122
-Q-.....126
-R-.....127
-S-.....130
-T-.....134
-U-.....136
-V-.....137

-W- 138
-Y- 141
-Z- 142
About the Author 143

It is good to be insightful , wise, intelligent, experienced, fair, honest, but never foolish in this Age of Cyber Terror.

Dedication

For my wonderful wife, Felicisima, and our brilliant daughter Mary. Thank you for inspiring me to always think deeply.

Acknowledgements

James F. Keenan, S.J.
Genrich Altshuller

Two People who have made a tremendously positive impact on our lives. Rev. James F. Keenan, S.J. for our understanding of Moral Wisdom and Genrich Altshuller for advancing our understanding of the challenge of Problem Solving.

Foundation

This work emerged from a lifetime of experience assisting organizations, teams, and individuals with finding inventive ways to solve problems more rapidly. As you move from country to country and culture to culture in search of inventive solutions to problems that are more common than one would ever imagine, you begin to notice several patterns emerge that reduce some of the mystery that shrouds the nature and character of human relationships including: How we form them; how we manage them; how we end them, and how we overcome them?

This is the stuff of life. Life is relationship living.
In Christianity, we believe in God as Relationship.

If you ask how I describe human life, I would answer you this way: Life is Relationship. For good or bad, from hope to hopelessness, from self-doubt to confidence, from Ego to Self-Esteem, and from life to death, I would tell you that human life is formed, nourished, developed, enjoyed, and even made miserable through relationship, from birth to death. From the day you meet your mother to the day you meet the undertaker you pass through life in relationship. Some of these relationships may be simply wonderful, but others may be Insider Threats who are actively plotting to steal from your company or perhaps even destroy it. Continuous Vigilance is the key to success. Lacking it, you will not maintain Continuous Performance nor Continuous Success. Here is the 21st Century, Insider Threat Prevention is the key factor in Continuous Performance Management.

How you manage your relationships says everything about how you will become a fully human person imbued with the capacity for living a life of significance. We are creatures with the capacity to reason well, true; but human life is considerably more emotional than rational. Rationality is a power we possess to navigate life on a material planet. However, we feel more than we think. We use reason occasionally to assist in decision-making, but use our emotions most often to navigate the experiences of our lives. Think about this:

> Reason concerns the rules of logic, but emotion flows from the values we hold dear. Emotions represent value judgments, and reason represents logical conclusions, if-then-else. The decisions we

> make based on value judgements we render often conflict with the decisions we conclude from deduction or induction. This is how we live human life on planet earth. Other places, I am not so sure.

All my life, Wise people have told me that the power of reason makes us human. We are the "rational animal". I guess, then, some people are more human than others. Does this make the artist less human than the scientist? Or, are we speaking about the human potential for rational thought so that the scientist is actually a human being and the artist is potentially a human being?

Moreover, the claim that human beings are "rational animals" is rather simplistic because human beings are more than animals, as Aristotle suggested. Although we do have the powers that animals share such as reproduction, self-mobility, growth, and so forth, we enjoy powers beyond those of brute animals like spiritual development, cultivation of virtue, and creative powers of the imagination.

How you manage your relationships says everything about how you will become a fully human person imbued with the capacity for living a life of significance. We are creatures with the capacity to reason well, true; but human life is considerably more emotional than rational. Rationality is a power we possess to navigate life on a material planet. However, we feel more than we think. We use reason occasionally to assist in decision-making, but use our emotions most often to navigate the experiences of our lives.

> This is the stuff of life. Life is relationship living. In Christianity, we believe in God as Relationship.

Think about this: Reason concerns the rules of logic, but emotion flows from the values we hold dear. Emotions represent value judgments, and reason represents logical conclusions, if-then-else. The decisions we make based on value judgements we render often conflict with the decisions we conclude from deduction or induction. This is how we live human life on planet earth. Other places, I am not so sure.

All my life, Wise people have told me that the power of reason makes us human. We are the "rational animal". I guess, then, some people are more human than others. Does this make the artist less human than the scientist? Or, are we speaking about the human potential for rational thought so that the scientist is actually a human being and the artist is potentially a human being?

Moreover, the claim that human beings are "rational animals" is rather simplistic because human beings are more than animals, as Aristotle suggested. Although we do have the powers that animals share such as reproduction, self-mobility, growth, and so forth, we enjoy powers beyond those of brute animals like spiritual development, cultivation of virtue, and creative powers of the imagination.

An animal has body, like a rock has material volume occupying space, but an animal is not a rock. A rock requires transitive motion through an external agent to move it, while an animal enjoys imminent motion from within to move itself. So, an animal enjoys the powers of a rock in having existence and a body, but exceeds rocks with its own many powers not enjoyed by rocks. In like manner, human beings possess powers not enjoyed by animals. Human beings are, in fact, beings governed by conscience and the Cardinal Virtues. While we do not call animals "self-moving rocks", we really ought not to call human beings "rational animals". We are considerably more than that.

The problem for human beings here is one of reconciling our emotional powers with our rational powers. It is more than a matter of being "rational animals or "emotional animals". Being more than rational animals who enjoy the power of emotional judgment, the question persists: What kind of creature are we if not a rational animal? What is the influence of virtue in all of this? Throughout their lifetimes, human beings experience multiple environments concurrently. As self-directed evolutionary beings, we share many of these environments in common with people around the world. We also experience these environments uniquely in ways that reflect our personal interests, commitments, beliefs, and aspirations as social beings. The three environments that most impact the development of this book and Parts that follow it are the:

- Via Virtutis, the Way of Virtue
- Via Inventiōnis, the Way Invention, Creativity, or Problem Solving
- Via Rationis, the Way of Reason, Structured Thinking, or Logic

I had thought about this ontological quandary for more time than I am willing to admit. Finally, I read a very find book about Moral Wisdom that quite artfully explained how reason meets emotions in human beings through the cultivation of insights about the Cardinal Virtues now seen as: Justice, Fidelity, Self-Care and Prudence. The author, James F. Keenan, S.J., presented a potent model of human behavior that distinguished between human weakness and moral failing. While we focus on the weaknesses, we mostly ignore our most serious faults like failing to do the right thing whenever possible such as the corporal and spiritual works of mercy. In his book, Fr. Keenan makes the fundamental argument that human beings are spiritual beings who become free only through the exercise of virtue.

To the extent that we fail to be virtuous beings, we deny our authentic humanity. Virtuous people are fully human and existentially free beings. Whether we are fundamentally rational or even emotional beings is the wrong question. Our description as fully human emerges from our commitment to the virtuous life. When you hear someone say that this or that person is without conscience and lacks all gratitude, you are hearing a description of an animal at work, not a fully free human person. Rationality does not make human nature fully human, it is the spiritual nature of the person that enables the human being to lead a virtuous life, and therefore, free life. In this way, we can say that a human being is a virtuous being who is made free by realizing virtue as a way of life.

As I began my career, I saved copies of everything I produced whether in college or at work. After several years of working as a senior product engineer in the computer hardware industry, I shared a Phased Development Methodology (PDP) I had produced with an engineering company down the street. To my surprise that company offered me $25,000 to purchase it outright. Fortunately, my manager from work happened to be with me at the time and suggested that I think about the offer for a while before jumping on it. After all, if they were willing to buy it outright for $25K what were they going to make off it? He had a good point. So, I did some research and learned what they wanted to do with it. As a result, I decided not to sell it and became a member of the software licensing industry instead.

In those days, organizations commonly employed formal development methodologies such as Phase Development Process (PDP) as the standard for their development teams. My methodology differed in that it was a methodology for designing methodologies. It was not just another methodology; it was a meta-methodology, a methodology designed to facilitate the design of methodologies. I conceived of it as a tool that assists software and hardware developers with designing methodologies that are more appropriate to solving their problems at work. I understood that success emerges from advances in methodology and this, in turn, requires meta-methodologies appropriate to the nature of the problems being solving. I further understood that advances in methodology required advances in Philosophy. Here are the Rules:

1. To be valid, a methodology must first be appropriate to the problem being solved.
2. Every advance in science was first preceded by advances in methodology.
3. Every advance in methodology was first preceded by advances in Philosophy.

This was the professional beginning of my career as a methodologist and a person who deeply wanted to simplify the problem-solving process. This is when I began to notice that many people experienced the same challenges with the same problems. The people may differ in each situation, but the problems were strangely the same. I found that many of my prior solutions resolved the situation quite nicely. I had already begun to build my Applied Intuitive Solutions™ Repository but had not yet realized it.

Throughout my career, I retained ownership of my work and devised ways to put my solutions to use in appropriate situations. I eventually developed a set of algorithms that enabled me to review transform my consulting deliverables into virtual solutions. After many years succeeding and refining my approach of rapid problem-solving, the hardware with sufficient power and speed finally arrived that permitted me to deliver a wide range of evidence-based solutions in real-time online.

The problem for me throughout this inventive process was to understand what exactly it was that I was building. Was it solutions in action? Was it solutions on demand? Was it intelligent solutions of demand? Was it evidence-based solutions? Was it rapid problem solving? Was it a new kind of E-Learning? Or is it Applied Intuitive Solutions™? Moreover, do my solutions reside in a repository? Or, do they form a component of a Knowledge Base System? What was it that I have developed over my many years of perseverance?

These questions have come at me over the years until last year when I made an accidental discovery. People refer to it as TRIZ, or, "Teorya Resheniya Izobreatatelskikh Zadatch" if you speak Russian. If you do not, the people from the Altshuller Institute refer to it in English as "Inventive Problem Solving." Although not identical to what I have been thinking, TRIZ shares some similar concepts.

Genrich Altshuller, working in Russia, began thinking about his ideas in a methodical kind of way about the same time as I did in Ohio. "Isn't life strange?" I am not going to contrast and compare the methods here. I acknowledge TRIZ for enabling me see that I, too, am engaging in "Inventive Problem-Solving" (IPS) using a variation of the problem analysis-solution generation approach described by Genrich Altshuller. This insight enabled me to more fully understand my own work as a specific type of Inventive Problem Solving that focuses on the behavioral and dynamic soft-skills category of problems.

Theoretical School & the Via Rationis

While developing skills as a meta-methodologist, new insights into the nature of problem solving continually emerged in the world around me. These were the Paradigmatic Case-Based methods of the mid-twentieth Century and beyond. In significant ways this "School" participated in the work of Genrich Altshuller whose interest predated them all.

While Altshuller focused on "Inventive" ways to solve problems using pre-existing solutions, members of the Theoretical School introduced the emerging power of computers, information sciences, and software to implement a potent kind of Case-Based systems more commonly referred to as Case-Based Systems and the Knowledge-Based Systems, Expert Systems, Executive Information Systems that followed. Although a list of noteworthy people contributed to the development of these technologies, not all were the pioneers that Herbert Simon, Marvin Minsky, and Janet Kolodner had become.

The authentic Pioneers were the people like Genrich Altshuller who broke new ground while working alone to introduce a new vision of problem-solving to the world and Herbert Simon and Marvin Minsky who introduced novel ways of thinking about technology as the framework for a new kind of Artificial Intelligence systems. As the ideas of the Pioneers emerge and take root, they attract a significant enough number of followers who populate the movements that become the industries of the future. In my lifetime, the people that contributed to the introduction of new problem-solving systems included:

- J.C. Shaw: Artificial Intelligence Languages, 1950
- Allen Newell: General Problem-Solving Systems, 1956
- Herbert Simon: Artificial Intelligence, 1956
- Edward A. Feigenbaum, Expert Systems, 1975
- Marvin Minsky: Stereotypes Based Reasoning, 1975
- Roger C. Schank: Dynamic Memory, 1982
- R.J. Sternberg: Intelligent Systems, 1984
- R. P. Hall: Artificial Intelligence, 1989
- Aamodt: Knowledge Based Systems, 1989
- R. Bareiss: Exemplar Based Systems, 1989
- R. J. Machado: Fuzzy Expert Systems, 1992
- Janet Kolodner: Case Based Reasoning, 1993
- Bruce Porter: Machine Reading & Artificial Intelligence, 1997

While Pioneers like the Nobel Prize winner Herbert Simon introduced new ways of using computing technologies in multiple disciplines, other people became associated with specialized systems and applications as highlighted below:

Exemplar-Based Reasoning Robert Nosofsky, 2016
Instance-Based Reasoning: Didier Dubois, 2002
Memory-Based Reasoning: Craig Stanfill & David Waltz, 1986
Case-Based Reasoning, C. K. Riesbeck & R. C. Schank, 1986
Traces-Based Reasoning, Alain Mille et al.., 2013
Analogy-Based Reasoning, Arkadiusz Wojna, 2005

The problem for me throughout this inventive process was to understand what exactly it was that I was building. Was it solutions in action? Was it solutions on demand? Was it intelligent solutions of demand? Was it evidence-based solutions? Was it rapid problem solving? Was it a new kind of E-Learning? Or is it Applied Intuitive Solutions™? Moreover, do my solutions reside in a repository? Or, do they form a component of a Knowledge Base System? What was it that I have developed over my many years of perseverance?

These questions have come at me over the years until last year when I made an accidental discovery. People refer to it as TRIZ, or, "Teorya Resheniya Izobreatatelskikh Zadatch" if you speak Russian. If you do not, the people from the Altshuller Institute refer to it in English as "Inventive Problem Solving." Although not identical to what I have been thinking, TRIZ shares some similar concepts. Genrich Altshuller, working in Russia, began thinking about his ideas in a methodical kind of way about the same time as I did in Ohio. "Isn't life strange?" I am not going to contrast and compare the methods here. I acknowledge TRIZ for enabling me see that I, too, am engaging in "Inventive Problem-Solving" (IPS) using a variation of the problem analysis-solution generation approach described by Genrich Altshuller. This insight enabled me to more fully understand my own work as a specific type of Inventive Problem Solving that focuses on the behavioral and dynamic soft-skills category of problems.

Systems Schools and the Systemists Who Built Them

General Systems Theory:

- Sociology: Parsons & Buckley
- Philosophy: Hegel
- Economics: Boulding
- Physiology: Shannon
- Mathematics: Weiner & Ashby
- Biology: Bertalanffy & Miller, Garard

First-Order Cybernetics:

- Mathematics; Ashby & Weiner
- Physiology: Shannon

- Information Theory: Weaver
- Computing: McCulloch
- Engineering: Prigogine
- Control Theory: Bateson
- Anthropology: Mead

Second Order Cybernetics:

- Biology of Cognition: Pask
- Experimental Epistemology: Maturana
- Family Therapy: Bowen

The Systems Sciences:

- Interdisciplinary Movements
- First-Order Cybernetics
- Science Studies

Systems Approaches:

- Management Cybernetics: Beer, Espejo
- Critical Systems: Jackson & Flood
- Critical Systems Heuristics: Ulrich
- Systemic Inquiry: Checkland
- Applied Systems: Checkland
- Systems Failure: Applied Systems: Checkland
- Information Systems: Stowell, Wood-Harper
- Systems Agriculture: Spedding, Badwen
- Social Systems: Buckley, Vickers
- Management Science: Ackoff
- Soft OR: Management Sciences, Ackoff
- Systems Analysis: RAND Corp.
- Management Learning: Schon, Argyris
- Systems Dynamics: Forrester, Meadows, Senge
- Whole Earth SD: Macy
- Systemic Complexity: Capra

- General Systems Theory: Bertalanffy
- Second-Order Cybernetics: Von Foerster
- Operations Research: Beer, Churchman, Ackoff
- Complexity Science; Ashby

These five environments, and the people that inform them, have contributed to the world we live in today. Their efforts will contribute to the future even more than they do now as Artificial Intelligence begins to impact society in even more potent ways. So, let me ask you two important questions:

1. Do you understand the impact that Artificial Intelligence may make on your life?

1. Do you understand that "intelligence" no matter the sources are never ever artificial. If humanity launches Intelligent Machines that evolve independent logical conceptualization actuality and powerful reasoning capabilities, but lack a foundation of Ethics, Morals, and Virtues that is compatible to the moral grounding of human society, significant dangers will emerge. It is a certainty. Caveat Emptor!

"I t's Not Very Often that You Get to See
Into the Development of a Cyber Terrorist.

Welcome

Welcome to a newer, simpler, and more effective way of navigating the professional minefield you call work. I dedicate this book to everyone who suffers from the assault of painful and ineffective colleagues. Whether you are a member of the Board of Directors or a new hire beginning your career, no one wants to work with colleagues who characteristically produce more turmoil than satisfaction and disaster than productivity.

I wrote this book for all of us who at some time or another had to snatch victory out of the jaws of defeat and overcome the "strangeness" of colleagues we could rarely understand. If you are a Millennial, this book is especially for you. If you cannot relate to such a situation, this book is really for you. I wrote this book for everyone who looks at their organization and murmurs: "This place really doesn't make any sense. I just don't get it."

Well guess what? A lot of people just don't get it, especially the ones who think they do. If you get it, answer me this: Are you the kind of person who should recruit other people to work with you? Are you good for others? Are you really a good person who should be invited onto a team responsible for producing critical deliverables? Simply put: Should people want you as a colleague? Will you be good for them, or only good for yourself? What do you think? Have you ever thought about it? If not, you probably already have your answer. Some people are not even good for themselves.

I wrote this book for all of us who are currently building our careers and for the generations who will yet follow in our footsteps. This book emerged to assist you with navigating the hidden influencers that energize the workplace. These are the sparks that make-or-break effective performance. These are the sparks that produce the painful or joyful lives we live. I tip my hat to all of us. Now let us get busy and achieve something great with our careers. Why settle for less?

Preface

Welcome to a new adventure in which Millennials, Cyber Terrorists, and Continuous Performance Managers (CPM) take center stage. As you race through these pages, you will find that this work transcends previous discussions about digital transformation in the workplace. As we proceed from one page to the next, please remember that while everyone has an opinion, not every opinion is an informed opinion. Perhaps this book can reduce this insufficiency. A critical mind, not a mind full of criticism, is the only prerequisite to this work.

Our journey through these pages spans an interesting selection of seemingly unrelated topics. You will enjoy quite a cognitive stew. We will begin with a few pounds of Existential Hunger adding a consideration of the kinds of relationships it forms. We next season with a pinch of Moral Wisdom, values, and virtues. Finally, to reduce any bitterness, we add a measure of Insider Threat Prevention and Human Activity Systems, with a reduction of organization design, performance management, strategic innovation, and professional growth. This recipe will satisfy your hunger for potent solutions to your own problems. Finally, following dessert, your will generate a number of new questions without building ill-will among team members.

Everything discussed in this work will never directly criticize any person, place, or thing. Never say never, right? The author simply discusses situations and events in a way that first enables us to better understand the challenges we face. We then seek potent courses of action to rapidly resolve them. This work encourages you to reframe discussions about Continuous Performance Management and Cyber Security as a more far-ranging topic of sociopathology than commonly envisioned.

Reading this book offers a real gift if you are up to it. The author designed this book to assist you with advancing along the path of becoming a potent human being as you build your career and manage your life. Many people slide by you know. They do the dance; they weave in and out of situations; they attempt to charm life and become the smooth operators that people sing about in pop culture, and they deceive their followers and fans. You see these people every day. They already think they have it made, that they have the right education to get them ahead in life. However, heads do roll and people sooner or later have to confront themselves. Ultimately when the conditions are right, these people feel the unease of the question that everyone has already asked about themselves a thousand times a thousand: "How human am I really?" No matter what, everything eventually ends.

In this current age, a time I refer to as the "Age of the Fragmented Rationality," many people enjoy their lives without a thought to how much wisdom has evaporated over the last twenty to thirty years. A number of these people have little idea about how much they are missing out on the substance of the truly human adventure found in a full life. It is a terrible tragedy to be unaware of one's capacities and skills and potentialities. It is likewise a terrible tragedy to be so consumed with so much stress for so long that the mind makes a wrong turn to get out of its own way. True, every age has its own advantages and disadvantages. Previous generations, however, valued more highly the things that made human life really human. This included things like morality, ethics, virtue, and oh yes, the discipline of really thinking well, that is, thinking well below the surface of the merely social conventions of dominant groups.

Here, you can pause for a minute, take a break, and think about yourself and your colleagues in a newer, freer, and certainly more potent way. You can learn more realistically how to connect your heart with your mind or your mind with your heart, healing the "substantial fragmentation" that is the reality of people today. Fourth, the work delivers the Moral Wisdom, skills, and expertise that enables you to gain better control over your professional life. Here, you learn to effectively navigate the one or two colleagues who bother you the most.

This work delivers a Moral Wisdom Process Model that enables you to cultivate and maintain potent professional relationships. Moreover, it enables you to navigate the dreaded social situations that impede your career. In sum, this work assists you with forming the relationships you should form, avoiding the relationships you should avoid, and exiting the relationships you should exit. Professional success in the Digital Age requires the in-depth Moral Wisdom that enables you to navigate sociopaths at work. I wrote about this in more detail in an earlier book. While this book focuses on Insider Threat Prevention, Moral Wisdom does not take a day off.

I designed this work to assist you with reducing the unnecessary complexity of your professional lives. This work does this in several ways. First, the work assists you with the recovery of the kind of lost social knowledge that makes human life more potent. Second, the work enables you to master an innovative point-of-view about professional life without starting World War III. Third, the work delivers the Moral Wisdom that enables you to change the direction of your life if you so desire.

I encourage you to think deeper and more profoundly about the issues you believe you understand while connecting your hearts and minds more humanely to the design of a more appropriate problem-solving process. This approach to problem-solving is the beginning of the process to become fully human because it breaks through the pre-suppositions that many people hold dear about the workplace without proper reason.

When contemplated with an open mind, this work delivers a challenging, thoughtful, and entertaining experience. The work raises several inter-connected topics in a fresh way so that you can expand your mind, not blow your mind. This work will expand your vision of the workplace as it requires you to focus on the issues discussed using a systems perspective. This work indirectly illuminates the career path ahead by presenting the opportunity to expand your vision-building capacities. However, you must energize your rational processes yourself. Mastering this work will enable you to escape the dulling world of everyday work life by reducing the emotional conflicts you experience while concurrently sharping your intellectual capacities. Life does not present such an opportunity every day.

Today people merely assume that they are human beings simply because their mothers and fathers probably were. However, it takes work to become truly human. A person has a right to constrain one's own existence, of course. Nevertheless, a person makes a great mistake, whenever he or she attempts to constrain the existence of another. Is it not more comfortable when human beings encounter other human beings along the journey called life?

Introduction to This Series

I wrote this series to address the dramatic challenge of Insider Threat Prevention Cyber Security, a much-ignored urgency in this time of Cyber Terror. The work began as a single paper about the dangers of Insider Cyber Threats, but the incessant questions of colleagues led me to see the need for a more detailed and expansive evidence-based work that can guide workplace practice. This series addresses The Psychology of Insider Threat Prevention in a practical sense by discussing the need to "Unify", not integrate, the CPM organization and Insider Threat Prevention discipline.

I chose Continuous Performance Management (CPM) as a platform for discussion for two reasons. First CPM is an extremely popular Human Resource Management model for organization design. Secondly, CPM vastly increases the danger of an Insider-generated Cyber Attack that can rapidly destroy an entire enterprise, and few seem to see this. I chose the Problem of Workplace Psychology as the overarching theme to tie the components of the "CPM-ITPCS Unification" Program together in a coherent fashion.

I have studied the problem of Insider Threat Prevention Cyber Security in the USA, Europe, Asia, the Middle East, Australia, and all points south for more than 50 years. In the beginning, no one called it Insider Threat Prevention Cyber Security. People used novel expressions I will not dare to repeat. When I speak of "prevention", I mean A Priori Prevention, prevention before a threat even requires mitigation. This is challenging. Part One discusses the pieces to the puzzle, Part Two discusses what to do what all the pieces, and Part Three presents a Unified Model of CPM and ITP Cyber Security. I use Behavioral Science and Psychology to clarify the depth of the problem and the range of the strategies available for delivering ITP CS.

I hope you find each Part stimulating as they become available. My goal was to remove the intellectual cobwebs that are so common today. Success with this requires curiosity, interest, dedication, abundant study, and practice. Insider Threat Prevention Cyber Security emerges as a Human Activity System in which the components are human beings. You know what this means right?

Human Beings are incredibly creative and unbelievably destructive. We have to be more creative and better enterprise designers. You will never have time to be bored.

Agony, If Nothing Else, Is Life's Faithful Retribution
for Entering an Ill-Advised Workplace Relationship

The Formative Questions

What Do You Deserve? Your career can be a rewarding life-long experience. It can be an enduring and wonderful gift. Or, it can become a dismal punishment whenever you ignore Moral Wisdom. Career success, however, is a lot like the weather: Everyone talks about it, but no one does anything about it. Sound familiar? So. what kind of career do you want? If you choose to accept a miserable situation, you may be the cause of your misery.

Where Do You Fit In?

Developing effective skills in Cyber Sensitive Environments requires a combination of soft-skills, hard-skills and personal qualities unimagined only a decade ago. University did not prepare you for this, but Moral Wisdom does.

A Few Relevant Terms

Moral Wisdom; Continuous Performance Management; Cyber Security; Insider Threat Prevention; Archetypes; Workplace Relationships; Resilience; Excellence; Existential Hunger; Applied Intuitive Solutions™; Knowledge Base Systems; Mobility; Human Activity Systems; Evolutionary Guidance; Design Inquiry; Coaching; Trust; Zero Tolerance; Invincible Ignorance; Cardinal Virtues; Sociopathology; Problem-Based Learning; Case-Based Reasoning; Evidence-Based Solutions; Traces-Based Reasoning; Unified Problem Solving Method; Unified Problem Solving Method Description Language.

1: Our Memory, Our Life

What Should We Remember

The memories we capture throughout our lives are quite something. Some are good and some are not so good. However, they are all ours. No other person has memories quite like we do. Yes, they may have similar memories. They may even enjoy, or not, shared memories. They may even be memories which we have developed together doing stuff together. Nevertheless, their memories are theirs. They are not our memories. Our memories are our memories. They are not their memories. We may even disagree over our shared memories. Disagreements over memories happen all the time. Memories are really something. That being said, it is nevertheless true that we all have memories that are unique to us. We each own our memories in ways that are unique to each one of us, even though they may be shared memories.

As I contemplate the nature of memories in general, I often wonder how precisely our memories capture the reality of the experiences we have indeed lived, have experienced, both the good and bad experiences, and even the dull experiences not much worth remembering. Think about it. It is quite something. People do experience many things in common and then remember them differently. We remember seeing different colors, different sizes, different angles, different places, different this and different that. We indeed remember a lot of stuff. Strangely, however, two people sharing the exact same experience even withing the exact same situation at the same time, will probably share very different memories about the collectively experienced situation. Simply amazing!

Even a single person will store memories differently based on how that person experienced a situation psychologically and factually. Was this person tired, sleepy, angry, indifferent, hungry, distracted, disinterested, over interested, deceptive, and so on and so on? Beyond ourselves, we face so many external effects that can further warp our memories. Just take a minute and think about this. There is something I need to say here but I cannot quite get it out. It's on the tip of my tongue. Ah yes, the "Google Effect" strikes again. You know what this is, right? Passive learning strikes again.

Have you ever been in a team meeting and you were aware that your turn to speak was fast approaching? You were the next in line! Ugh. While a colleague was still speaking, you were thinking about your "script", but then your boss "out of nowhere" asks you what you think about the current remarks just made by your colleague. Could you remember these remarks? He or she just made his or her remarks, and you do not remember them except for perhaps only one or two words. Simply wonderful. WOW! How can this be the case? Well, you were the next in line, weren't you? Where was your attention, on your colleague or yourself? Malcom Brenner (1973) would say that your attention was most likely on yourself and what you were going to say.

This is the "next-in-line" effect. This is the tendency to forget information that was said immediately before your turn to speak because you are distracted by preparing what you will say next. This happens due to limited attention resources being diverted to preparing for your own performance, resulting in a failure to encode (process) the preceding information properly. The effect was first experimentally demonstrated by Malcolm Brenner in 1973, using a task where participants took turns reading words aloud and were later tested on their recall.

Beyond this, we can ask ourselves about how much time we spend strengthening, and also, refining our personal ability to remember something and then recalling it later. This, of course, focuses on the development of our capacity for learning. Today, with the omni-availability of the Internet, the capacity of many people for learning and recalling is declining, not growing. They have become passive learners. The Internet has actually increased the human need for active learning and memory testing to strengthen one's long-term memory. Perhaps tis is a good time to consider a few of the psychological and technological roadblock to communications and learning that people have to overcome today to achieve understand and agreement to form potent teams and, of course, professional and social relationships. So, let us begin with the Absent-Minded Effect. Or, have your forgotten already what I am writing about here? Do yourself a favor, and don't be so absent-minded.

The Absent-Mindedness Effect

Have you ever been accused of being Absent-Minded? Many of us have at some time or another. I think, but it is only a guess. I forget. I wish I would have paid more attention. I am trying to remember but I am not thinking deep enough. I suppose that I am trying to do too much right now. The distractions are getting the best of me. I've got to focus, focus, and focus. My age is getting to me. I will be 23 soon enough. Ha. Ha. Sure, I will. I would certainly do better if I could learn to take my recall to a deeper level of semantic processing. Obviously, my phonemic process won't do it for me. Obviously, the context of the information matters. I suppose that my memory would improve if I could only learn to drop the suffix. Apparently, these is indeed something to that so-called "Suffix Effect".

My Echoic Memory used to be good enough. Now it has become a hinderance. Apparently, my serial memory will not be good enough for the work ahead. I need to know much more than a few items here. I must place the more important information upfront or at the very end to improve my recall. I also need to be better at PLC. It certainly cannot do any more damage. Obviously, I need to improve my ordering skills because my recency and primacy effects seems to have changed priorities. I often forget the first item on a list but have little trouble remembering the last item of a list. Thank goodness I don't suffer much from Memory Inhibition but when I do, it's more helpful than hurtful.

Psychology of Insider Threat Prevention

An individual's psychological and emotional dispositions, states, behaviors, and experiences strongly influence the learning approaches and reactive behaviors of an individual to the contingencies of Insider Threat Prevention (ITP). For example, while some people remember information better from an auditory presented list, other people remember information better whenever they receive such information from a visually presented list. Such a preference defined Modality Effect" is, indeed, a psychological phenomenon. We are psychological

persons strongly influenced, perhaps even influenced, or perhaps governed, by psychological desires. For example, you only need to consider the psychological phenomenon referred to as "Duration Neglect" to understand what I mean. In this case, the length of an experience has little impact on a person's overall retrospective evaluation of it. Isn't this interesting, right? It appears that our memory of an experience is disproportionately influenced by the peak experience and the final moment of the experience. Peak and Final, this is it. This is another gift of psychology.

Now think about what this means when we are in meetings about the design of confidential security approaches for preventing or reducing Insider Threats. Often the people in charge of these meetings present unusually long lists of information about ITP methods and approaches. This is great for some people. However, for most people, the "List-Length Effect" (LLE) reminds us that "the proportion of correctly recalled items decreases as the list size increases.

More specifically, Murdock, 1962) warns us that the proportion of correctly recalled items decreases as set-size increases but at the same time the total number of recalled items continues to increase with set-size. Some research over the years has suggested that recall accuracy decreases as a function of increasing list length due to increased interference and decreased positional and temporal distinctiveness in longer lists.

Even without this research, we all know that long list equals increased forgetfulness while short list equals reduced forgetfulness. It seems that long lists are scare many people. As a psychological trait, especially in Insider Threat Cybersecurity, the "Serial Recall Effect" reminds us that we will remember the information at the beginning and end of a long list more so than we will remember the info in the middle. This is interesting because a lot of the elderly people I have known have told me that they can remember their earliest years and latest years better than they can remember their middle years. Perhaps, this is why the "Serial Recall Effect" as a primary operating rule of memory reminds us to place the most important information at the beginning and end of a presentation or even on a list rather than in the middle where it will most likely get lost.

Today, especially in the Age of Social Media information becomes distorted and then embedded in the mind as fact following a specific event. Thus, in the minds of some people, falsehoods become the new truths. This "Misinformation Event" can become so embedded in a group that realty become distorted to the extent the events that never occurred become the new dogmas of decision-making. Obviously, since human memory is do malleable and creative, we have to be extra diligent when working through important situations that have wide spread ramifications form humanity in small and large groups. When you add to this problem of Misinformation, and the psychological challenges of the cognitive processes of "Leveling and Sharping", you can see that existence is peppered with many tarpits and pitfalls.

Moreover, this Leveling and Sharpening cognitive process is supplemented by the psychological heuristic referred to as the "Peak-End Rule." Through this process, people make judgements about an experience based on its most intense point combined with its end point, or conclusion rather than considering the entire experience. One can see here that people generally discard the specifics of a situation and adopt the generalities of that situation. Similarly, people forget the negative emotions associated with a memory much faster than they forget a positive emotion. Psychologists refer to this as "Fading Affect Bias."

Being human does not always come so easy for so many people. This is because we all have so much psychological and behavioral challenges to overcome every single day. Just when we begin to think that we have mastered the great mysteries of the COSMOS, we find another challenge waiting for us right around the corner of life. Human being, in general, are faced with the difficult challenge of overcoming their negative biases, prejudices, stereotypical biases, implicit stereotypes, implicit associations, spacing effects, false memories, suggestibility,

Cryptomnesia, misattribution of memory, source confusion, and so many other psychological manifestations that impact reasoning, values development, judgment, moral development, virtue adoption, decision-making, goal attainment, social commitment, commitment, attitudes, empathetic behaviors, ethical reasoning, relationship formation, personal integrity, one's sense of fairness, one's sense of fairness, generosity, consistency in thought and action, self-discipline, love of self and neighbor, sense of self-control, and so many more characteristics of human life govern and enabled by one's psychological states. Obviously, human beings are indeed human being are formed and governed through the states of their psychological development, emotional or not. All of these characteristics influence in some way to focus on the things we indeed focus on.

For example, our Negative Bias compels us to focus on the negative experiences of our lives that often influences our perceptions of reality in irrational ways that assault of well-being. Obviously, we have to shift our attention to focus on more positive things. It is a good practice here to change all of this by adopting special practices such as engaging in mindfulness, displaying gratefulness, focusing on positive experiences, and shifting attention. The goal here is to enhance positivity as much as possible and enhance one's mental health. since this kind of shift is indeed difficult to make, I cannot stress enough here the need for people to make every effort possible to shift to a more positive state. Paul Rozin and Edward Royzman remind us that negativity states are very difficult to overcome. They impact social interactions, and emotions, and generate unpleasant thoughts, harmful events, and traumatic events. This negativity effect is seriously debilitating. You see, this is just a single manifestation in the development of a person's intrinsic and extrinsic psychological states. Obviously, one's psychology state is an extremely potent and influential force in the life of every person. Many people are not as free as they would like to be. Their own psychology holds them prisoners.

Think about Prejudice and the challenge of Stereotypical Bias. Wow, what a problem this can be! Prejudice is a preconceived irrationality that negatively impacts attitudes and judgments. Negative without adequate knowledge it involves "prejudging" someone before knowing him or her as an individual. Hence, we find people involving themselves on assuming things about other people based on race, religions, education, gender, age, wealth, health. We can thank prejudice for gifting us with mean-spirited discrimination. Human Psychology strikes again, but in a negative way.

As Prejudice can become, we can still behave even worse towards other people. We do not have to stop with prejudice. We can also Stereotype individuals, friends and strangers alike, and often do so. Stereotyping is a double-edged sword. It results not so much from a deliberate sense of maliciousness but from some level of memory distortions that generate indefensible beliefs about targeted groups of people based on the usual discriminator groupings including race, gender, educations, income, religion, weight, height. This cognitive bias often manifests itself as some kind of psychological problem such as constantly confusing the names of certain people from different genders, races and/or economic levels. This kind of bias can be very uncomfortable for both parties because it is associated with the distortion of a person's memory.

As one can gather from these psychological manifestations, Prejudice and Stereotypes generate a wide range of interpersonal difficulties that are not based on "good vibes". The last few pages have introduced a number of impediments to forming positive and healthy relationships. In many ways, this stuff is i and requires much thought and hard work to control and eliminate even if one wants to eliminate it. Unfortunately, this is only the beginning of the psychological challenges human beings experience. We really have to roll up our sleeves and get to work. Humanity deserves the effort. For example, how do we address Implicit Stereotypes and Implicit Associations? Many well-educated people have not even heard of them. They are associated with many other psychological effects that can harm oneself, friends, family, and strangers alike. For example, are you familiar with Implicit Stereotypes and Implicit Associations?

Insider Threat Prevention (ITP) & the Omnipresent Biases

Think about the confusion generated by the psychological complications mentioned above. It brings to mind three common words: "What a Mess!" You see the problem here is that not only the Cyber Terrorists, the Cyber Criminals, are complicating the lives of the people in the organization, but the people, themselves, often become part of the problem because of their own psychological stereotypes and biases. More times than one would imagine, the good people become suspects and the bad people become trustworthy team members of the insiders or guests for the outsiders.

Corporate life has become more challenging today for many hard-working employees because the security and control of the corporate Information Technologies have become the current urgent focus of the C-Levels with more riding on the outcome as never before. After all, the most trustworthy person in the organization often turns out to be the Cyber Terrorist next door kind of person. Even a few of the C-Levels themselves have occasionally been found to be the great betrayers, the great Insider Threats who were not prevented from carrying out their hidden plans nor recognized until the damage had been done. It happens.

To be successful, Insider Threat Prevention, as it involves "prejudging" someone before knowing him or her as the individual he or she actually is rather than simply as just another member of a work group, requires the introduction of extensive controls, procedures, standards, specialized technologies, processes, and security experts place in sensitive places throughout the organization. Beyond this, organizations will continually require the design and implementation of ever more rigorous controls and security solutions.

Insider Threat Prevention is the new "Never Ending Story". It is difficult enough to catch the Cyber Criminal among us during the best of all situations, but when you add the psychological constraints and impediments, things really become challenging. Think about the Cyber Security challenges facing us today without all of the psychological baggage if you can. It is difficult. Let's continue our Cyber Security Mission with the understanding that Human Psychology is at the forefront of the Cyber Security challenge.

As we use the Tools and Techniques that are available to us today, we can work continually to make them more robust and appropriate to each Cyber Security situation that we encounter in the organizations we support. For example, consider the Implicit Stereotypes and the Implicit Associations among us. These biases are deeply unconscious and influence perceptions and actions about the people among us in the workplace, and even elsewhere. Thankfully tools such as the Implicit Association Test, the IAT, are available that enable us to measure the implicit biases that we hold so dear and yet that remain so well hidden. It seems that we all have attitudes about the groups that surround us everywhere, from politician to police officers and from clergyman to candy man, and even from workmates to bosses. No one gets a pass. The psychological reality we face is bitter-sweet: We all face unconscious attitudes and beliefs that may influence our thoughts and actions. They operate automatically without our conscious awareness and may even assist or impede our actions to deliver a robust Cyber Security program. Apparently, the word implicit preceding the psychological process actually means implicit when it comes to the effects of human psychology on Insider Threat Prevention.

It is worth recognizing that so much of our attitudes about life are shaped by our very own cultural experiences, the environments we live in, our parents and schools, and how we were raised by our parents. The important fact to remember here is that implicit means implicit. It means exactly what it says. These unconsciously experienced psychological events may differ considerably from the explicit beliefs that we all consciously hold. Beyond these implicit psychological effects, we also alter some memories after the fact. This occurs through a long list of effects including:

1. Spacing Effect
2. Suggestibility
3. Fale Memory
4. Cryptomnesia
5. Source Confusion
6. Misattribution of memory
7. Incorrect source
8. Suggestibility
9. Factors contributing to misattribution
10. Sleep deprivation
11. Brain activity
12. Overlapping information
13. Workplace Conflicts
14. Too Much Information
15. Misattribution of memory
16. Availability heuristic
17. Attention bias
18. Illusory truth effect
19. Mere exposure effect
20. Context effect
21. Cue dependent forgetting
22. Mood congruent memory bias
23. Frequency Illusion
24. Baader-Meinhof Phenomenon
25. Empathy gap
26. Omission bias
27. Base rate fallacy
28. Bizarreness effect
29. Humor effect
30. Von Restorff effect
31. Picture Superiority effect
32. Self-relevance effect
33. Negativity bias
34. Anchoring
35. cognitive bias

36. Conservatism
37. Conservation Bias
38. contrast effect
39. Distinction bias
40. Focusing effect
41. Framing effect
42. Money illusion
43. Weber-Fechner Law
44. Confirmation bias
45. Congruence bias
46. Post-purchase rationalization
47. Choice-supportive bias
48. Selective perception
49. Selective perception
50. observer-expectancy effect
51. Experimenter's bias or Experimenter's Effect
52. Observer effect (sometimes called the Hawthorne effect
53. Expectation bias
54. Ostrich effect
55. Subjective validation
56. Continued influence effect
57. Semmelweis reflex
58. Bias blind spot
59. Naïve cynicism
60. Naïve realism
61. Confabulation
62. Clustering illusion
63. Insensitivity to sample size
64. Neglect of probability
65. Anecdotal fallacy
66. Illusion of validity
67. Masked man fallacy
68. Recency illusion
69. Gambler's fallacy
70. Hot-hand fallacy

71. Illusory correlation
72. Pareididolia
73. Anthropomorphism
74. Group attribution error
75. Ultimate attribution error
76. Stereotyping
77. Essentialism
78. Functional fixedness
79. Moral credential effect
80. Just-world hypothesis
81. Argument from fallacy
82. Authority bias
83. Automation bias
84. Bandwagon
85. Placebo effect -
86. Out-group homogeneity bias
87. Cross-race effect
88. In-group bias
89. Halo effect:
90. Cheerleader effect:
91. Positivity effect:
92. Not invented here:
93. Reactive devaluation
94. Well-traveled road effect
95. Mental accounting
96. Appeal to probability fallacy
97. Normalcy bias
98. Murphy's law
99. Zero sum bias
100. Survivorship bias
101. Subadditivity effect
102. Denomination effect
103. Magic number 7+2
104. Short-term memory
105. Illusion of Transparency:

106. Curse of knowledge
107. Spotlight effect:
108. Intrinsic incentive
109. Illusion of external agency:
110. Illusion of asymmetric insight:
111. Consistency bias
112. Restraint bias:
113. Projection bias
114. Pro-innovation basis
115. Time-saving basis
116. Planning fallacy
117. Pessimism Bias
118. Impact bias
119. Declinism
120. Moral luck
121. Outcome bias
122. Hindsight bias
123. Rosy Retrospection
124. Telescoping effect
125. Less-is-better effect
126. Occam's Razor
127. Conjunction fallacy
128. Delmore effect
129. Law of Triviality
130. Bike-shedding effect
131. Rhyme as reason effect
132. Belief bias
133. Information Bias
134. Ambiguity bias
135. Status quo bias:
136. Social comparison bias
137. Decoy effect
138. Reactance
139. Reverse Psychology
140. System justification

141. Backfire effect
142. Endowment effect
143. Processing difficulty effect
144. Pseudo-certainty effect identified by Kahneman and Tversky.
145. Disposition effect
146. Zero-risk bias
147. Unit bias
148. IKEA effect
149. Loss aversion
150. Generation effect
151. Escalation of commitment
152. Irrational escalation
153. Sunk Cost fallacy
154. Identifiable victim effect
155. Appeal to novelty
156. Hyperbolic discounting
157. Peltzman effect
158. Risk compensation
159. Effort justification
160. Trait ascription bias
161. Defensive attribution
162. Fundamental attribution error
163. Illusory superiority
164. Illusion of control
165. Actor-observer bias
166. Self-serving bias
167. Barnum effect
168. Forer effect
169. Optimism bias
170. Egocentric bias
171. Dunning Kruger effect
172. Lake Wobegone effect
173. Hard-easy effect
174. False consensus effect
175. Third person effect

176. Social desirability bias
177. Overconfidence effect

Wow, we have a lot of self-development ahead of us if we want to master ITP and minimize the threats involved. We really need an appropriate approach. Perhaps some shared insights are worth the effort.

Some Insights Worth Considering

Please understand that Insider Threat Prevention is a fluid process because every threat is fluid. The perpetrator can change his or her threat profile rapidly. It is worth remembering that ITP entry points are so numerous because every person is more unique than you would ever imagine. This uniqueness enables them to design threat protocols that may challenge even the most experienced Cyber Security expert. ITP defends do well to when they become proficient at becoming a Critical Source Evaluator, a CSE. This means that the CSE absolutely must be engaged in a continuous process of learning to master the art, science, and skill of ITP. This is a challenging responsibility, but it is not boring.

Think about the long list of psychological biases and manifestations above. It is complicated, right? It is a daunting list that reminds us of the complexities involved in Insider Threat Prevention. Unfortunately, the long list above is only a partial list of the biases, prejudices, stereotypes, and psychological reactions that ITP specialists confront as they attempt to counter the Insider Threat incursions. Obviously, when it comes to ITP, an organization must always be on guard and in a defensive mode of behavior. Moreover, the ITP teams must also learn to protect themselves from their own psychological short-comings. ITP is such a fertile field of ideas and strategies. Sometimes we miss important clues because of our own psychological tendencies. With this being the case, we do well to learn how to protect ourselves from the Insider Threat Perpetrators and from the psychological tendencies of ourselves. For example, consider the origin of your memories, especially about critical information. Then review explicit, clear, accurate, and comprehensive documentation to accurately record ITP contributions and note ITP decisions. After this, design and implement errorless and clear communication protocols to ensure accurate attribution of ideas and actions. Moreover, continually be mindful of your own tendencies and continually verify the origin of your memories, particularly when they involve important ITP events or decisions. Finally, consistently overcome the biases and related psychological tendencies listed above.

2: Newkirk Axiom

> It is the responsibility of every person to do something positive every day to make his or her relationships more enjoyable every day. Getting up every morning and committing oneself to living better than the previous day requires an extraordinary way of thinking informed by a specific kind of potent wisdom. The only way anyone is ever going to be able to meet such a commitment to his or her relationships is by knowing more each day about the stuff that really matters. The only way anyone is going to know more about the stuff that really matters is if someone shares this knowledge. This is the why and how of joyful relationships. Learning it all by oneself has never happened, and never will. If anyone could do this, it would take too long. When learning to navigate sociopaths at work, time still matters, especially in a Cyber Terror world.
>
> We all need someone and someone always needs us. This is the first principle in forming potent relationships. It is about them, not us. We find ourselves through our capacity to form mutually positive relationships with other human beings. Relationships matter, and enjoyable relationships matter most.

A colleague recently mentioned that he enjoyed reading my blogs. "But what's the point?" he asked. "What value do they offer to people in the corporate environment?" My colleague is a great man with an in-depth understanding of physics, law, and political science. He has keen insight, possesses a highly developed intellectual capacity expanded by vast experience, and enjoys a creative perspective on life. In short, he is no slouch. When he speaks, I listen.

His are fair questions, I thought, deserving of fair answers. Well-versed in Newkirk's Law 4,129, "The Law of Irritating Possibilities," I recognized that if he felt this way, many people will feel pretty much the same. If my law is accurate, and you know it is, I must provide "good enough" answers that respond to my colleague's veiled plea for relevance. I cannot adequately complete such an undertaking, however, in a single paragraph. I must take care to add some pot-roast to the potatoes.

This book, therefore, makes a special effort to answer my colleague's questions. Here in Chapter One, I will begin clarifying the message of the previous chapters in Part One by exploring the nature of positive workplace relationships and their impact of human performance, and possibly malicious insider threats. As you proceed along these next few chapters, you will be able to see quite clearly the influence that relationship skills have on executives, managers, and everyone else in the work-place. This includes you and me, and, of course, my colleague who started all of this by questioning the relevance of my blogs. It also includes especially those who eventually emerge as malicious cyber threat actors.

We Are Every Person

If you would sum up my previous publications, you would find that I generally wrote about topics that impact the lives of human beings as individuals. These topics spanned topics such as the hidden impact of character, the power of insight, necessity for attaining higher values, potent rationality, essential morality, art of being fully human, leadership, nothingness, and other things. Each publication implicitly whispered a plea to remind people to remain attentive to what they are doing to become the persons they are continually becoming.

My plea went out to executives, politicians, and the other important people who seem to control the destiny of everyone else in this society. Mostly, however, I intended my plea to inspire the minds and hearts of the unrecognizable background masses. These are the people whom we daily pass without notice. These are the people who suffer the slings and arrows of the outrageous fortunes of a contemporary life made more difficult by the executives, politicians, and other important people who may be the masters of the ship we sail into the future.

The interconnectedness of life reminds us that what we do and who we become can impact many millions of people we will never meet. Every human life instills profound meaning in every other human life. In this way, "We Are Every Person". The joy, pain or terror people suffer impact us because we recognize that it could be us, and it is us.

Where we are, the families we enjoy, the people we suffer, the careers we build are a mystery of life. Why am I anyone? Why are you not someone else? The answer is not merely the luck of the draw or the transmission of delicate chemicals. Think about it. The answer is vitally a cosmological unfolding. Intimately, the questions are about relationships.

Communal Humanity in the Workplace

Human life is about relationships. We come into the world through the painful efforts of a mother who was assisted by others, from physicians to mid-wives to taxi-cab drivers and firemen, and even occasionally bumbling husbands. From day one, we begin life as creatures of relationships. Isolation is not normal for the human being. Our birth is the most crucial moment in our lives, and it is characterized by relationship, most notably the mother and child relationship.

We spend much of our time in the office wading through or avoiding all the baggage that people thrust upon us from their private lives. Obviously, we have to be cautious about the depth of relationships we form in response to the legacy relationships of our office mates.

The list of external relationships influencing our professional lives in the workplace is immeasurable. This list includes difficult husbands and wives; corrupt friends; poor bosses; noble project managers; dedicated workers; lousy politicians; terrible doctors; strange families; rising stars; liberal religious leaders; conservative authorities; brave soldiers; terrifying terrorists; weak minded intelligentsia; steady workers; positive stalwarts; shining stars; iconic leaders; brilliant innovators; Intellectual Property thieves; religious converts; atheists; social radicals; leading-edge path finders; saints; mystics, Cyber Terrorists, and all the rest.

All of these people may in some way influence the relationships we navigate at work. Regardless of the colleague you work with, you can be sure that you will enter into one of the many kinds of relationships that define the social environment. This is the totality of human life. Life is a relationship with the living and a memory of the past. Every problem has its root in some kind of relationship problem. Study the chapters forming this book to better understand how you can develop and maintain potent relationships in the workplace. Discover how the models in the series may guide your success in the corporate world. To gain a better sense of what my colleague was talking about above, you may want to read the subsequent books in this series about the Psychology of Insider Threat Prevention Cyber Security. In the meantime, think about what this book is saying to you about the Psychology of Insider Threat Prevention. Use this time to deepen your professional insight and learn how to more rapidly navigate sociopaths at work. This is the best way to prevent insider threats.

Now we go on to Chapter Two where we begin to explore the Hallmarks of successful Insider Threat Prevention Cyber Security. Such a Program enables organizations to re-thing their strategies and focus on a wide range of topics in innovation, project management, business design, Information Technology, E-Commerce, and so forth to improve performance in the workplace or further develop competence in any given area.

> Life is Relationship Living. Life is a synergy after all in which one relationship impacts another in the continuous and ever-expanding spiral of human life.

3: Existential Hunger

Relationships play a pivotal role in the development of an individual throughout a person's lifetime. From cradle to grave, relationships form and enrich human existence as the individual learns to become fully human. As an employee in a large organization, you may occasionally become too busy to think about what you are doing. When this happens, you need to slow down, focus on the current situation, and think about something intelligent. For example, if you genuinely want to learn about navigating the people in your organization, learn something about the nature of their core relationships. In this way, you will gain a significant amount of knowledge about the people working with you. However, if you want to learn an invasive amount of information about the people around you, this will tell others a lot about you.

In the 13th Century, St. Thomas Aquinas observed that if we are genuinely interested in knowing another person, we must come to know what that person loves. It is never enough simply to learn what a person does or listen to what a person says. Learning about relationships reveals everything about human love, in and out of the workplace. Knowledge of what a person loves uncovers the deepest character of the person. Moreover, this knowledge of love reveals the level and influence of Existential Hunger on a human life and the formative substance of the relationships it forms.

Existential Hunger in a Life

My question for you: What kind of relationships do you hunger for? Yes, we human beings hunger for relationships. Nursing Infants hunger for their mothers. Older children hunger for their parents and occasionally for their friends. Young adults hunger for relationships that satisfy their ego-needs. Older adults should hunger for much more substantial relationships than those of children. Sadly, many adults, even more mature adults, remain driven by the hunger of self-centered desire. This is the hunger of a young child. It is ego-centric, completely.

Reason, values, morality, ethics, and faith collectively influence the relationships we form throughout our lifetimes. They are the "core influencers of life" and are inescapable, even in the courtroom where moral arguments are seen as aggressive. They are the key forces that make us the kind of person that we are in the process of continually becoming. The thoughts we think, tenants of faith we believe, values we hold, decisions we make, virtues we practice, and actions we take at work in relationship with other people emerge from the impact that our relationships have on us and we on them.

Dimension Two: Core Influencers of Life

Collectively, our core influencers energize our public and private actions and inform our private and public statements. Our depth in living, knowing, caring and discerning is actually quite communal and leads us to respond to life in ways that will always be subjective, anxiety prone, and authentically religious, even for the atheist and the anti-religious progressive who advocates multi-species marriage and the cloning of God Himself. Interestingly, our core influencers of life are formed in community with other people, emerging from the relationships we either enjoy or dread as emergent shapers of life itself.

Throughout a large expanse of our lives, our rationality, values, morality, ethics, and faith do not belong only to us. Much of the time, we do not even know how we gained our most cherished beliefs and values. They enter our hearts and minds even before we know they are there to influence the rest of our lives. We carry these interjections into the workplace and become the kind of manager or colleague we reveal to the team, especially when we try to be someone else.

People go through life without ever questioning the core influencers that point them down the paths they take. They merely go where they go because it merely seemed like the thing to do. The road came up before them and they followed. Since they have not yet set a path for their journey, any path was good enough. Some commentators of the social scene claim that many people form the relationships they do merely because this is where life has led them, whatever this means. Work, home, play, all chosen without in-depth living? Even horses and cats have stronger wills then this.

Life, of course, is more deliberate for human beings than this. Being different from cats, butterflies, tilapia, grasshoppers, and ostriches, well maybe not ostriches, we spend a lifetime experiencing the different levels of Existential Hunger that compel us to form the relationships we do, about four principal levels of existential hunger. Our progression through the four levels of

Existential Hunger have much to do with the kinds of people we become, the relationships we form, the joys we experience, the disappointments we suffer, and the perspectives of life we cherish.

You might say that our experience moving through these four levels of Existential Hunger, prepare us for the relationships we experience while not forcing us into them. We have to build or destroy our relationships ourselves. It is one of the powers we have as human beings. The experiences we accumulate as we pass through the four levels of Existential Hunger form our world views, our Weltanschauung as the philosophers say. How is your German?

You can begin to see the impact that the core influencers of life have on your professional behavior and the relationships you build outside of the workplace. Believe me when I tell you that whenever you are in the workplace, all of you is there, even when you are daydreaming. Your daydreams, after all, are a part of you. So, dream well to earn your pay.

We are now ready to discuss Level One Existential Hunger, the level of Existential Hunger that complicates the lives of adults. All of us have to outgrow Level One Existential Hunger if we ever wish to gain the respect of colleagues and friends. The effects of Level One Existential Hunger (L1EH) become more pronounced as people ascend the corporate ladder. Indeed, if you are a manager still battling the influence of L1EH among your colleagues and employees, they deserve all the pity you can give them, which probably will not be much.

Although L1EH is common among young children, as the first developmental stage of life, plenty of adults are still stuck at this level every day of their lives as a developmental challenge. In extreme cases within the workplace, everyone suffers because of this fixation, from the manager to the receptionist, from the customer to the stock holder. L1EH is devastating to teams in the workplace. While thinking about this, you may want to purchase a new car, some DVDs, a new T.V., go on a vacation, get a new suit, maybe two or three, and pick up a new computer along the way. A new car would not be bad either. Some of you may like this idea; others may think it is crazy. In the remainder of this chapter, I will tell you why.

The Core Influencers of Life:

- Reason,
- Faith,
- Ethics,
- Morals, and
- Values

L1EH and Objective Relationships

So far, we have been discussing the impact of the core influencers of life on executives, managers, and other people in the organization. Earlier, I stated that human reason, values, morality, virtues, ethics, and faith all influence the relationships we form throughout our lifetimes. These influencers are the "core influencers of life". They are inescapable, even in the courtroom where moral arguments are seen as aggressive.

Level One Existential Hunger

We have seen that human beings confront and manage four levels of Existential Hunger and that each level of Existential Hunger informs its specific range of relationships. For example, people experiencing L1EH, not a medical condition, commonly form objective and manipulative relationships. L1EH people fail to develop the noteworthy virtues while they exaggerate other core influencers such as self-interest.

> L1EH is so compelling because it encourages people to think only of themselves, often at great cost to other people.

From the foregoing, we can see that people at the first level of Existential Hunger are normally young children. Adults at L1EH are fixated at the emotional level of childhood. This is the first insight of the Newkirk Model of Human Relationships (NMHR): Adults in the workplace at LIEH are self-centered. Their favorite words are "I want". Time for your first surprise quiz:

> Question One: Why do human beings have so much trouble achieving good and healthy relationships? Hint: Consider the level of Existential Hunger that characterizes the colleagues in the relationship. L1EH aligns with Objective and Manipulative Relationships. That's it. L1EH

Relationships are never fun, unless you despise yourself, and then you are probably exaggerating your internal inconsistencies, which is what people generally do when they describe themselves with malice. Although this law may be simplistically obvious, it remains difficult to follow. Even in the 21st Century, bad relationships are more common than good ones.

> Newkirk's First Law for Insider Threat Prevention: Pay attention to the good relationships at work and even more attention to the bad ones. Insider Threats take both forms.

Although this law may be simplistically obvious, it remains difficult to follow. Even in the 21st Century, bad relationships are more common than good ones, but the good ones can be threatening also.

Objective Relationships

The relationships of people suffering with L1EH, not a medical condition, are objective to the extreme. L1EH people see other people as objects to be judged. For L1EH people, every relationship is an objective relationship. L1EH people form Objective Relationships to analyze, criticize, take apart, rebuild, redesign, categorize, and summarize other people. L1EH people do this from a safe distance that provides a barrier against intimacy.

In Objective Relationships, high ego and low self-esteem dominates. These L1EH people stand off and study their peers, colleagues, and "friends" impersonally as objects of curiosity. L1EH people rarely engage in positive interaction with colleagues since they are mere objects. "Demand and Judge" is their approach to life. Judgment is the defining transaction of the Objective Relationship and occurs exclusively between the subjects and objects forming the relationship. For people handicapped by L1EH, outsiders do not exist in any meaningful way. Outsiders are received as unwelcome interlopers who may upset the status quo.

Adults functioning at L1EH are noteworthy for their desire to demean the value of human life. They label other people through episodes of impersonal judgment. They behave as if the L1EH person can grasp the infinitude that is another human being. L1EH personalities see other people as simple objects only fit to be used in the pursuit of satisfying the private desires of the L1EH personality.

The language of Objective Relationships is quite uninteresting. One might call it dull or boring. Adults who suffer from L1EH judge everyone dropping countless labels such as flakes, extremists, conservatives, liberals, know-nothings, hypocrites, things, good-for-nothings, simpletons, bums, obstructionists, pot heads, disappointments, trouble makers, racists, idiots, blockheads, patriots, progressives, lawyers, suckers, and on and on.

No one can be all of these things unless of course they enter politics. It is worth noting that a large population of managers prefers to form only objective relationships through which employees are the objects of productivity. "Isn't life strange?" The Moody Blues got this much right. In these one-way Objective Relationships, feelings run deep when the objects ultimately realize their status. Analysis and judgment provide the energy that keeps L1EH people going. After all, if we cannot analyze and criticize our friends and politicians ad infinitum, what good are they?

People who remain fixated at the ego centric L1EH see human beings coldly and with an "as a matter-of-fact attitude" that is intended to deceive. For the L1EH person, human beings are not sacred beings of cosmic value, but are either convenient or inconvenient means to ends, either useful or redundant objects of analysis and criticism. What else can they possibly be?

> For the L1EH Personality, human beings are never ends in themselves, rather they are means to an end.

Pervasiveness of L1EH People

People fixated at L1EH come from all walks of life. They belong to every political party and probably worship with every religious denomination. L1EH people are equal opportunity criticizers. They criticize everyone equally without any distinction to race, gender, religion, age or sexual orientation. Being so closely connected to everyone, they judge and criticize them all. They are indeed equal opportunity criticizers. The EEOC would love them.

Since L1EH people are common in the workplace, you do not need to look very hard to find them. Worry not, they will find you. Can you imagine what a relationship with L1EH Personalities must be like? Doubtlessly, they would be objective for sure. With these people, you are the object of the invectives that never stop. Do you understand now why you may want to find another job if your boss is fixated at Level One Existential Hunger, plagued with a high ego state drive ignited by childish desires?

Type One Existential Hunger: Ego Centric

- Objective
- Deceitful
- Manipulative

Level One Existential Hunger

L1EH and Manipulation

As the L1EH people begin to move on to more complex desires, they begin to construct relationships that enable them to move from judgment to manipulation. Understanding that they cannot obtain everything they want by working alone, like great wealth or recognition, they enlist the assistance of people to facilitate their desire to have even more stuff. "Having it all" is their goal. Their highly perfected skill of "Level One Judgement" prepares the L1EH Personality for the inevitable art of manipulating colleagues to serve their personal needs by becoming extensions of the L1EH Personality.

This expanded approach to L1EH relationship building results in the Manipulative Relationship. This relationship exists whenever the L1EH Personality uses the other party as a tool of needs satisfaction. In forming the common Manipulative Relationship, the TOEH Personality manipulates colleagues to sacrifice themselves for the benefit of the L1EH Personality, regardless of the cost or inconvenience to the colleague. Being such an expert judge of people, because the manipulator has practiced judging other people so thoroughly by building Objective Relationships, the L1EH Personality knows who to enlist in their schemes of avarice run wild, the inexperienced, good-natured, eager, and unwary person new to the art of manipulation.

A later chapter will examine the Manipulative Relationship in more depth. There you will see that Manipulative Relationships are a one-way street to professional torment. Sadly, people fixated at L1EH are ill-equipped to form any other kind of relationship. Getting beyond L1EH requires a deeper level of Existential Hunger than is possible for individuals at the L1EH level suffering from fixated emotional development. We will address this matter later.

As you can doubtlessly gather from the discussion so far, executives require a large capacity of discretionary judgment for the people they invite into the management ranks, or hire to lead Insider Threat Prevention Cyber Security programs. The reasons for this caution, though, differ considerably from the reasons normally offered by Human Resource Management organizations. Because of the level of Existential Hunger that drives them, a significant number of people are capable of forming only objective or manipulative relationships, no matter what. This is one of Newkirk's Laws of Observation. Think about it, deeply.

> Newkirk Law of Observation 37: Level One Existential Hunger Generates Relationships that engages in the behavior that rapidly satisfies L1EH.

L1EH constrains and directs the behavior of the relationship. L1EH is a high ego hunger for stuff, emotional or material. As such, it generates relationships that accommodate the high ego drive for accumulating more stuff. Obviously, the core influencers of life have not fully kicked in for L1EH person in a way that is consistent with a fulfilling life.

The rationale for the actions of the L1EH Personality is driven by a high ego state with low self-esteem. The morality, ethics, and faith of these L1EH Personalities are singularly twisted to satisfy their wants, needs, and desires, their (WNDs). These WNDs influence the nature of the relationships they form over the course of their lifetimes. Their high ego state combined with their characteristically low self-esteem forms the core influencer of their lives. The fixated drive of self-centeredness is the key force that forms an individual to behave as L1EH personality. With the right inducements, these people make excellent cyber criminals because their consciences are so poorly formed.

The thoughts they think, the depth of faith they practice, the values they hold, decisions they make, and actions they take in the workplace in relationship with other people emerge from the impact that their relationships have on their colleagues and we on them. Collectively, their immature core influencers energize their public and private behaviors and inform their private and public statements.

Unlike other people, their depth of maturity in living, knowing, caring and discerning is actually quite isolated. It leads them to respond to life in ways that will always be ego-centric, manipulative, and inauthentic, even for the popular leader and the socially progressive person who advocates multi-species marriage and the cloning of God.

Interestingly, the core influencers of the L1EH personality are formed in community with other people, mostly their immediate families. Like us, they emerge from the relationships they either enjoy or dread as emergent characteristics of life itself. This emergence may represent significant emotional growth or may generate a fixated state of self-centeredness that eventually comes to present to the world an adult with a child's emotional drives. Negativity, aggression, and defensive behavior characterize the workplace environment of relationships whenever they emerge in response to the L1EH personality, see below:

Supervisor versus Employee:

- Negative Assumptions
- Self-Protective Behaviors
- Observed Aggressive Behavior
- Negative Assumptions
- Self-Protective Behavior
- Observed Aggressive Behavior

In summary, the L1EH Personality is characteristic of people who are fixated at the high ego and low self-esteem states of behavior, the states customarily manifested in young children. The L1EH behavior manifests itself as episodes of objectification and manipulation through which the L1EH personality attempts to manipulate people as a tool of self-fulfillment and personal acquisition regardless of the cost to the colleague. The strong drive of the L1EH Personality to lose oneself in the accumulation of more stuff weakens his or her personal identity. Naturally this further weakens the potential for growth and ignites an "I want it all" type of existence, no matter what.

People today spend an inordinate amount of their time craving objects of technology. Eventually, they then use these objects to ignite an even deeper high ego hunger for stuff such as public recognition, good or bad, and personal power, also good or bad. Why not, they argue, since they are now connected with the world and everything they do is well "liked" by someone somewhere.

Fixation at L1EH is a bad situation for everyone in the organization sine L1EH Personalities are capable of only two principal kinds or relationships, the objective and manipulative. You would be wise to avoid both of these kinds of relationships whenever you can. If your boss suffers from L1EH, you will need a survival strategy at the least or you would be wise to move on elsewhere to something bigger and brighter in your life. Believe me. You do not want to be part of a colleague' Objective Relationship or the victim of your manager's Manipulative Relationship. Now we will look more deeply into the Manipulative Relationship to learn how to better manage such a relationship if we are in one, or avoid it altogether if we can.

Manipulative Relationship

As L1EH people grow out of their judgment prone stage of life, their High Ego driven hunger begins to evolve, adapt, and become ever more virulent. Sadly, when this adaptation occurs, the L1EH person becomes even more proficient at using other people to get what they want. They easily forge relationships in which their colleagues and other workmates become the means to their desired ends. Even though the L1EH Personality has graduated from objective relationships to manipulative relationships, they, nevertheless, still suffer from the high ego state level of Existential Hunger. The problem here is obvious. Although human beings have moved from targets of judgmental assaults, they have become targets of needs fulfilment. This even sounds more horrible.

People who have not yet moved beyond their L1EH fixation are painful to be around. They are real pains to those who have gone on to enjoy the other levels of Existential Hunger more appropriate to their age of development. You need to understand the limits of the L1EH Personality who become your manager: When you work for a L1EH Personality, he or she will relate to you impersonally. In their eyes, you are, after all, less than human. Your only value is your utility. In short, you have become the means to the fulfilment of their ends. You are not yet an end in yourself, you have been objectified. This is the first step in becoming a member of a Manipulative Relationship.

It is characteristic of the Manipulative Relationship that a high ego person manipulates people in the relationship to satisfy his or her own private needs, regardless of personal cost to the other. Moving beyond mere judgment to manipulation, high ego persons remain separate from colleagues and other members of the workplace relationship to erect barriers and constrain access. The L1EH personalities simply manipulate people to satisfy their needs, regardless of the need or the urgency of it.

> The Law of Paradoxical Manipulation: Manipulative Relationships only exists because the High Ego person judges that other people in the relationship are more capable than themselves.

The hidden message conveyed in the Manipulative Relationship is that the other persons in such relationships are more potent than the High Ego members. The High Ego member needs other persons to satisfy their personal needs. However, their low self-esteem actually tells us that they view themselves as inferior in many ways.

The High Ego person will say whatever they believe is required to convince another person to deliver what is desired. Manipulators like this keep their thoughts "close to the vest," but work hard to get you to tell them everything you can about a topic that has interest to them. Such people will get close to you but never let you get close to them. A Manipulative Relationship is an emotional one-way ticket, and you will have to pay the fine.

People in every walk of life entertain Manipulative Relationships at some time or another. You do not have to be a sociopath to form one. You should merely be a person fixated on L1EH. This is where every human life begins, in a relationship characterized by the child's Level One Existential Hunger. For infants and very young children, L1EH is quite normal. For adults, however, L1EH is quite chilling.

I do not recommend working for anyone at L1EH. Can you image what a Manipulate Relationship is like when every person in it is fixated at L1EH? We are back in Pre-K. Can you imagine the chaos? What if everyone wanted the exact same things? Would not this be interesting? Think of the possibilities. Now think of your organization. Chances are, you work with people like this every day, but have adjusted to the situation. After all, they need you on their side. You may be able to give them what they want.

At times like these, it is good to dust off the ole resume. People enter Manipulative Relationships every day. Operating in stealth mode, L1EH people do not call these relationships as manipulative. They call them jobs, marriages, friendships, programs, projects, congregations, units, families, organizations, classrooms, and anything else that may come to mind.

To Ignore the Psychological is a Formula for Failure

If you are well-grounded in the core influencers of life and actually live by them, you would already know what you need to know to avoid or manage these types of sociopaths at work. There is something vital about the core influencers of life that simplify complex situations and clarify life. Passage from L1EH to Level Two Existential Hunger (L2EH) enhances one's experience of the core influencers of life and enables people to enter more fulfilling relationships.

Chapter Three discusses Level Two Existential Hunger and examines what L2EH means to executives, managers, and other people in the workplace. People experiencing L2EH more often enjoy positive workplace relationships. They find more enrichment in life as they are free to master their occupations. They also become able to contribute more significantly to the organizations they serve. Join us as we continue to explore this fascinating topic, the Psychology of Insider Threat Prevention Cyber Security. We continue with the discussion about the levels of Existential Hunger and the sociopaths you meet in the workplace in Chapter Three.

Do you understand why Objective Relationships exists and eventually give way to the paradoxical implications of the Manipulative Relationship? People in Objective Relationships are greatly dissatisfied individuals who feel incomplete because they lack a lot of stuff. The stuff can be anything from money to power to fame. The desire for stuff drives their behavior and defines their self-worth. L1EH Personalities are forever dissatisfied with life. L1EH Personalities transform their dissatisfaction into judgmental and critical behaviors as part of their strategy for obtaining more stuff.

The tendency to think primarily about satisfying one's self-interested desires appeals to many people, especially people in leadership positions in business and government. If you stretch your hearts, you can hear them now: "Why think about anyone else when my self-interest is the overriding interest of my life?" This argument has a certain ring of satisfaction. Superficially it is attractive to the brute beast in each of us. Like the brute of raw nature, many people believe that they come into this world to pursue their own self-interested desires. What else would they do? What other reason makes sense to them?

Of course, the challenge of authentic love changes everything. So do the existential problems of relationships, communities, ultimate self-identity, cosmic universals, dimensional existence, immorality, expanded awareness, identity transcendence, infinite substantiality, apparent self-interest versus authentic self-interest, and the fact that people who love only themselves have fools for best friends. For people with L1EH, indifference to empathetic understanding becomes a grave deficiency. Exaggerated self-interest and the crucial development of empathy have remained antithetical to one another from the dawn of human reflective self-awareness, and that is a very long time. When these two influencers come together, something has to give. I do not see this situation changing any time soon, regardless of the musing of our politicians and the lectures of a few of our moral leaders in religious communities around the globe.

People fixated at L1EH have already made the choice: Exaggerated self-interest it is. If you care to bet on it, you would win every time. Now you can understand why L1EH Personalities excel in Manipulative Relationships? They have mastered the art of taking care of themselves at the expense of other people. The big question for us here, of course, is how does this happen? More importantly how can we protect ourselves from such people? As a first step, you need to recognize the Objective and Manipulative Relationships and then avoid them whenever you can. Ultimately, you need to learn how to navigate sociopaths at work. We are never as unique as we think we are and never as common as others claim we are. People who love only themselves have fools for best friends. Life is an organic Model fashioned by the Human Heart.

Never let somebody who adds very little to a relationship,
control so much of it. – Unknown

4: Level Two Existential Hunger

In Part One, we began to design a new model of the enterprise by examining the Psychology of Insider Threat Prevention Cyber Security and its Unification with Continuous Performance Management. In Part Two, we continued by examining the Problem of Sociopathology and its influence on the nature of workplace relationships using the Newkirk Model of Existential Hunger.

Although the concepts and terms used in this Model are mine, they offer much more than an interesting and orderly academic description of human relations. Realistically, though, Existential Hunger (my term) is something that energizes all of us as we attempt to maintain a firm grip on reality. That is, if we want to make it through life in a worthwhile manner.

If you have read Part One and are paying attention to Part Two, you will have noticed that this work calls upon a large number of seemingly disparate disciplines to present its subject matter and make its arguments. The problem with disciplines, however, is that they establish artificial boundaries that to focus attention on a specific knowledge domain mostly set apart from others knowledge domains. In this light, then, Geology is separate from Physics and Physics is separate from Chemistry, and Chemistry is separate from Biology, and Biology is separate from Mathematics. Not really.

Everything is in flux and all sciences are connected as a single reality in confluence. For example, is chemistry separate from biology and biology separate from mathematics and mathematics separate from astronomy and is this separate from physics? Where does one begin and the other end, and is this separate forever? Disciplines make knowledge and discovery manageable but also incomplete. Categories are artificial. This is the nature of the problem we have with Insider Threat Prevention Cyber Security. We need to transform a number of disciplines into a single knowledge base to deliver an effective Insider Threat Prevention Program. What disciplines can make this knowledge base possible?

It's not only Enterprise Architecture, Business Process Redesign, Governance and Risk Management, Cyber Security, Software Engineering, Business Management, Strategic Thinking, Product Development, Project Management, Finance, and Hardware Engineering. It is also about Behavioral

Science, Clinical Psychology, Sociology, Training and Development, Quality Assurance and Control, Data Management, Operational Planning, Recruiting, Operations, Philosophy of Science, Logic, Ethics, and many more.

Insider Threat Prevention Cyber Security is difficult. Getting it right involves several disciplines working as one. When organizations adopt Insider Threat Prevention Cyber Security (ITPCS) in environments that conflict with its practices, such as Continuous Performance Management (CPM), the Program becomes even more complicated. This generates an additional complexity that requires the Unification of CPM and ITP CS through the design and delivery of an enterprise architecture that is both simple to maintain and effective. The delivery of such an Insider Threat Prevention Cyber Security environment requires the mastery of behavioral, technical, managerial, and financial disciplines as a single coherent discipline appropriate to resolving the challenges of Insider Threat Prevention Cyber Security in a CPM environment.

Sometime ago Abe Maslow wrote about the "Hierarchy of Needs," as a common-sense approach to human behavior. His words offer admirable wisdom. However, I think we have to worry more about the impact of L1EH on our lives and the associated "Hierarchy of Desires" it encourages. Desires impact human behavior more than needs. People go astray because they desire more than they need.

Human beings generally desire more than they need. Notice that I said "generally". There are people on earth who have learned how to live for need rather than desire. I believe we call them monks. Some people work hard to fulfil their desires at the expense of their needs. Many others, ignoring their needs altogether, join the "desires chase". People choose their desires over their needs whenever they are free to do so. If they are not starving to death or fleeing terrorism for the sake of their lives, people will follow their desires to oblivion as if they were following a wild hoard of Lemmings over a cliff.

The pursuit of desires characterizes the life of those who fail to ascend through the higher levels of Existential Hunger. The freedom to pursue one's desires more than one's needs marks the difference between life in the First World and existence in the Third World. The former pursues desires, the latter survival. Whether one lives in a First World country or a Third World country, Existential Hunger still guides the self-development path through life.

This situation begins to change dramatically as a person moves from L1EH to L2EH. As one moves from L1EH, the drive of fulfilling the desire to have more stuff becomes subordinate to the deeper and broader interest in becoming fully human, reaching beyond oneself to find oneself in cooperation with other people. L2EH is genuinely transformative in this respect: Rather than focusing on the ultimate desire of "having it all," the person now wants to become more functional as a human person among equals.

This emerging perspective presents a major shift in attitudes about life. Here we begin to see that L1EH constrains our development as a fully functioning member of a human community. L1EH constrains our deeper creativity by continuously unleashing desires for stuff that inevitably restrains us from becoming ourselves. As St. Francis of Assisi would remind us, the more we own, the more it owns us.

The human being longs for authenticity. Such authenticity requires personal freedom, a type of freedom that cannot exist through L1EH because it sacrifices the person to the dictatorship of manipulation and the emotional isolation of the self from other human beings who have been objectified by the L1EH relationship.

Level Two Existential Hunger (L2EH)

As we grow out of our high ego state, we begin to see other people as they are. We begin to see that other people deserve the same rights and opportunities as ourselves. Here, at the second level of Existential Hunger, L2EH, people become subjects of potential rather than objects of manipulation. Type Two Existential Hunger manifests as Goal Directed Hunger in three classes of relationships. These are the

- Functional Relationships
- Project Specific Relationships, and
- Teaming Relationships

Through L2EH (not a medical condition), people experience the desire to be something significant, not just have something significant. Here human beings reach out to other human beings more effectively in new and more potent ways. Authentic creativity becomes more compelling in balancing the dynamics of communal life expressed in workplace relationships. People now hunger to improve their lives in more enduring and meaningful ways.

In grave disappointment to the commercial world, the desire to accumulate stuff diminishes. Indeed, the word "hunger" itself becomes inadequate to explain the new dynamic that characterizes the higher-level behavior of human beings in professional relationships which are themselves inspired by this higher state of Existential Hunger.

Human consciousness has changed dramatically during the ascendency to the expanded potential of L2EH (not a medical condition). Everything looks and feels better. Life becomes more enjoyable as tensions balance themselves with a new reality that frees the person to be more creative and more sincere without fear of criticism. People grow beyond L1EH attracted by the more noble desire to be someone and accomplish something significant for and with other people. This is Level Two Existential Hunger, L2EH. Through Level Two Existential Hunger (L2EH), we become highly functional human beings and boldly go where L1EH has never gone before, and never goes.

The most common words in the language of L1EH are: "I, me, I want, I need, you will, and you had better". In complete departure from the dull vocabulary of people fixated at L1EH, the most common words in the language of L2EH is: "We, together, our, depth, growth, development, functional, meaningful, us, you, expansion, fullness, gentleness, peace, understanding, please, restlessness, forward, positive, relationship, better, infinity, thank you, you have my gratitude", and such words that convey a movement from the single high ego state to a high sense of self-esteem reaching out to humanity in general.

L2EH persons express sentiments that convey a movement from the single ego to a reaching out to humanity in general. People who achieve L2EH progress from hyper self-concern to concern for colleagues deserving of respect rather than manipulation. L2EH signifies that a person has grown considerably beyond childhood and has begun the process of becoming a more communal and collaborative human being.

Working for managers at L2EH, rapidly improves one's professional life. Moreover, working with colleagues at L2EH offers the kinds of workplace relationships people enjoy. At L2EH, you have ceased being an object of judgment, analysis and manipulation. Rather you have become a serious contributor with your colleagues. Your status as a human being provides expanded participation in the corporate community.

In an environment influenced by L2EH, your managers and co-workers will ask your opinion about important, non-trivial issues and then seriously consider your response. Growth to L2EH, after all, merits the use of both your mind and you mouth. Previously, neither mattered much, only your compliance and obedience. After all, back then you were working for adult aged children who were still fixated at L1EH and had objectified you as candidate for manipulation.

A significant perk of your growth to L2EH is improvement in the quality of your workplace relationships.

While you gain admission to some of these relationships by invitation only, you will gain admission to others simply because you are a contributing member of the team. You form these workplace relationships simply because you have made the arduous journey from object to subject, from the outside world of forgetfulness to the inside reality of human possibilities. The new territory of your life will surpass anything you have experienced before simply because you are now working with people who have made the leap to adulthood and what matters most in life. You have formed Functional Relationships.

We most associate these relationships with L2EH and emotional enrichment. At the level of Existential Hunger, we move beyond the manger's adolescent, but nevertheless hurtful, compulsion to manipulate people around him. Although the name of the Functional Relationship has an impersonal ring to it, things only seem this way.

Functional Relationship

The Functional Relationship is far superior to any relationship possible with people fixated at L1EH. The more you ascend the levels of Existential Hunger, the more you enjoy the ethical dimensions of life. However, the more you remain fixated at the lower levels of Existential Hunger, the less likely you are to live an ethical existence. As we have seen, Existential Hunger strongly influences our development and the kind of workplace relationships we form.

These first three chapters of this book began to organize the Newkirk Human Relationship Process Model of Workplace Relationships. They discussed how relationships play a pivotal role in our development as human beings. In Part One in The Psychology of Insider Threat Prevention Cyber Security, we have discussed perennial human hunger and its link to the "influencers of life." We expanded on these themes by examining the first level of Existential Hunger, a high ego and low self-esteem hunger. Here in Part Two, we have progressed from a discussion of the Manipulative Relationship to L2EH and its associated relationship, the Functional Relationship. We will now take a closer look at this relationship to better understand why it is superior to both Objective and Manipulative Relationships, not a daunting task when considering the characteristics of the high ego state and low self-esteem relationship.

Functional Workplace Relationships

Unlike Objective or Manipulative workplace relationships, the Functional Relationship signifies the beginning of the authentic relationship. Functional Relationships are made for the workplace. Here people relate to each other as subjects of collaboration, not objects of manipulation. They link themselves with a common goal that is beyond the aspirations of any single human being. The objectification common among L1EH has evaporated. No one at L2EH suffers isolation or segregation since every colleague is equally accepted, and needed. In the Functional Relationship, people only differ by recognized and respected roles. Type Two Existential Hunger consists of three primary relationships:

- Functional Relationship
- Project Specific Relationships
- Teaming Relationships

Functional Relationships work well in project settings where the project manager works close with each person in the relationship. For example, the project manager works smart to keep the goals fresh and challenging. Although judgment and manipulation are common among relationships dominated by L1EH, they are counterproductive for people involved in Functional Relationships. Unlike relationships scarred by L1EH bitterness, Functional Relationships form as management works closely with other persons in the workplace relationship to attain common goals of performance and success.

We characterize Functional Relationships as communal and distinctive. People fill specific or distinct roles equally as colleagues who share a strong sense of togetherness to achieve common and overarching goals. The clearly defined roles and responsibilities of each person enable everyone in the Functional Relationship to gain a deeper understanding of all the people in the relationship and also of themselves.

The L2EH relationship is about as good as relationships get in the corporate environment. Though not impossible, rarely does an employee experience anything better. Nevertheless, many people achieve quite a bit of success whenever their managers remember that they themselves are members of the Functional Relationship and co-contributors to overall team performance. Functional Relationships compel managers to position themselves as members of their own teams. In this respect, they avoid making personal attacks of team members, and never objectify or manipulate their people.

It is impossible for L1EH people to form Functional Relationships since high ego state low self-esteem personalities cannot consistently collaborate in a functional manner. L2EH, of course, means that a person has outgrown the Existential Hunger characteristic of the L1EH inadequacies. Members of Functional Relationships are generally comfortable with the demands and potential of L2EH because this level of Existential Hunger compels one to abandon his or her sole focus on the satisfaction of High Ego state desires. Through L2EH, therefore, people become compelled to reach out beyond themselves to achieve deeper meaning in their careers by living fuller and more complete lives.

L2EH and Capability Maturity Models

The impact of Existential Hunger on business operations is astounding. It has implications for the entire organization. For example, technical people speak about the Capability Maturity Model (CMM) as a way to evaluate the potential for technological brilliance in an enterprise. People engaging in CMM audits review a wide range of assets, specifications, practices, and capabilities. Rarely do they consider Functional Relationships as a prerequisite to attain a high CMM rating.

Before the CMM Model becomes a tool of high performance management, however, organizations require Functional Relationships to establish an environment in which CMM makes sense. This will not occur well when an organization is plagued with a large number of people stuck at L1EH. Potent Functional Relationships are the prerequisite to CMM reliability because people must first possess the capability and maturity to engage a CMM environment.

Functional Relationships, of course, require human beings to reach out and seek fuller expression of their lives by being something more than they were yesterday. CMM fails when managers prefer L1EH sociopaths over the more potent Functional Relationships formed through L2EH development. It happens. Unfortunately, as we have learned by now, people fixated at L1EH have become so common in modern technologically driven organizations where people are valued most often as means to someone's ends rather than as ends in themselves.

Making the leap from L1EH to L2EH enables managers to build performance to the levels necessary to achieve high performance results. Moving from L2EH to Level Three Existential Hunger (L3EH), however, further enables people to build and enjoy even more fulfilling relationships. While L2EH frees people to contemplate the broader issues of corporate success such as the relevance of Capability Maturity Models for high-tech organizations, L3EH Existential Hunger inspires people to journey beyond the ordinary, beyond the goal of everyone else to experience a new openness resulting in a more profound life.

In Chapter Four you will learn that L3EH refers to behaviors that enable people to move beyond the hunger for growth that characterizes L2EH. T3EH compels people to seek the transcendent experience. L3EH is less corporate, personal, and rarely noted in organizations. When it exists, however, wonderfully creative things may occur that benefit the entire organization. L3EH inspires people to enhance their relationships in every environment. Here, growth becomes a virtue, a good habit. Here the habituation of virtue becomes pronounced. A fully human life becomes an ethical life. Moral philosophers equate the habit of ethical conduct with good health. They remind us to develop the habit of acting ethically before our health begins to break down. Obviously, the art of living a fully human life requires the cultivation of a spirit full of energy. It's Good to be in a relationship! After all, you cannot blame everything on God and Government!

5: Level Three Existential Hunger

Welcome to Chapter Four in Part Two of our series about the Psychology of Insider Threat Prevention Cyber Security. Examining Existential Hunger so far, we have seen that we can associate each level of Existential Hunger with a specific kind of workplace relationship. While Level One Existential Hunger produces Objective and Manipulative Relationships, Level Two produces Functional Relationships. An Existential Hunger Model of Relationships works in a manner such that the type of Existential Hunger (EH) generates specific kinds of relationships.

The equation is simple:

Existential Hunger Level (EHL) = Type of Relationship (TR).

This is a very simple equation, but very powerful. This is the power of a strong equation: Keeping factors simple but not under-conceptualized. However, simplicity is only the beginning. Each level of Existential Hunger generates a specific kind of relationship that is characterized by the human behaviors that emerge from that relationship. This follows from the fact that each level of hunger has its defining characteristics. Level Three Existential Hunger, too, has its defining characteristics.

Level Three Existential Hunger (L3EH)

Focusing on Level One Existential Hunger, we discussed the high ego state and low self-esteem hunger that compels people to constantly desire more stuff. The stuff could be anything from money to power. We also discussed the higher hunger for growth that compels human beings to become fully functioning colleagues at work. We have seen this realized through Level Two Existential Hunger. Additionally, we have seen how these three levels of Existential Hunger influence the development of workplace relationships.

We have also seen the impact that relationships have on the performance of an organization and the well-being of colleagues. Obviously, L1EH is detrimental to performance while Levels Two and Three are performance–centric in that they compel human beings to achieve something more significant with their lives than the accumulation of stuff.

While L1EH focuses a person on the mere satisfaction of unending high ego state desires, the L2EH focuses on commitment to and participation in the achievement of commonly shared goals with colleagues in goal-directed relationships. The focus of L3EH, however, is far beyond personal desires, shared goals, or even shared objectives.

L3EH compels people to move beyond the ordinary concerns of everyday struggles and experience the deeper meaning hidden in the ordinary and extra-ordinary events of life. L3EH compels people to seek emotional enrichment through spiritual connections that are beyond value and price. T3EH relationships are enjoyed by "beyond people," the people who see what is possible beyond the ordinary.

People experiencing L3EH are "beyond people". They never settle for mediocre relationships but test new boundaries of possibilities. Such people are creatively committed individuals who have grown beyond the need for games and intrigues. They mean what they say and do what they promise. L3EH compels people to reach out to experience the transcendent mysteries of life. Only mature adults experience this type of hunger, people who have become fully human.

Characteristics of L3EH Relationships

The characteristics of people living out L3EH serve as positive motivators of growth and self-guided evolution. They see creativity as a calling of the heart, a genuine vocation. They are receptive to going the distance and moving into unchartered territory and away from the routine situations that mark a more common life. People caught up in the excitement of L3EH are restlessness people.

They desire to find deeper meaning in life by experiencing relationships of depth and achieving states of genuine self-forgetfulness guided by the safety of a hard-won wisdom that frees the imagination to realize the possible.

Guided by the ethical demand for a higher life, people enjoying this much deeper connection with life strive to be needed and remain open to other people and novel situations. They become more discriminatory in the use of their time but never discriminate against other human beings in the exercise of their attitudes. Since such people live in a profound manner, they only make ethical connections. Casual relationships are rare in L3EH.

Unlike L1EH and L2EH, L3EH is energized by its ethical and religious dimensions. Obviously L3EH surpasses L1s and L2s in several important areas. For example, L3EH transports people beyond personal interests and common goals to encourage spiritual growth, connectivity, openness, and profound living in a way not ever envisioned by individuals living with the more basic types of Existential Hunger. It is the L3EH relationships that make life really enjoyable. Unfortunately, L3EH relationships are very rare in the corporate environment.

Summary

We have examined, albeit briefly, Objective, Manipulative, and Functional Relationships. We have considered the impact each has on life in general and more specifically the character of each in the workplace. From what has been presented so far, you require little intellectual effort to see that Functional Relationships are perfect for workplace settings. Here Functional Workplace Relationships affirm the value of each person in the relationship by expanding each person's sense of purpose. Only two relationships exceed the Functional Relationship in generating connectivity among the partners of a relationship. One, of course, is the Personal Relationship emerging from L3EH. The other is the Religious-Spiritual Relationship. This fourth relationship is appropriately associated with Level Four Existential Hunger, L4EH. Chapter Six examines the nature and characteristics of the L4EH relationship.

6: Spiritual Relationship

Welcome to Chapter Five. We are discussing Existential Hunger, the "core influencers of life" and their impact on the Psychology of Insider Threat Prevention Cyber Security. The first four chapters continue the exploration began in Part One where we discussed the Newkirk Model; Insider Threat Prevention; Continuous Performance Management; Sociopaths at work; Existential Hunger; Cardinal Virtues; and the relationships produced by Existential Hunger. We also discussed the idea of perennial hunger and its link to the "influencers of life." Here in Chapter Five, we discuss the Personal-Spiritual Relationship (P-SR) as it is associated with Level Four Existential Hunger (L4EH).

Personal-Spiritual Relationships at Work

Level Four Existential Hunger represents a great leap forward in each person's development. During this stage of personal development, we begin to live human lives more fully by entering into very profound relationships. Moving beyond the first three levels of relationships, people experiencing Level Four Existential Hunger (L4EH) begin to experience a more intense interpersonal level of intimacy that characterizes Personal-Spiritual Relationships.

While relationships enable people to share their existence with others, Personal-Spiritual Relationships expand the extent to which one person enters a state of "togetherness" with another. In this sense, then, the Personal-Spiritual Relationship is the most dynamic and creative relationship people can enjoy at work. Human beings do not create Personal-Spiritual Relationships. We simply accept or reject them based on our own spiritual depth. At L4EH, people more fully experience the sharp contrast of human emotions.

L4EH relationships are never lukewarm. Human beings either suffer terrible discomfort or enjoy great satisfaction from them because Personal-Spiritual Relationships can be positive and transcendent or negative and regressive. As a higher-order relationship, Personal-Spiritual Relationships commonly function as embedded relationships consisting of dynamic processes that lead people to experience every kind of relationship imaginable within a single relationship. Because of the intimacy common to them, people of L4EH experience relationships that carry them from the valleys of disappointment to the highest summit of joy.

> Personal-Spiritual Relationships are double-edged experiences. Although they form a significant part of the process of becoming a fully human being, they often cut us to the core.

The best and worse things in life occur as we experience the richness and challenge of Personal-Spiritual Relationships. For example, when these relationships are positive, they provide the palliative environment that facilitates healing. Such healing, however, only occurs in the relationships that have emerged out of commitment to a working alliance. Moreover, these alliances succeed only when people abandon their high ego state attitudes that generally set people against each other. This kind of emotional growth, therefore, enables human beings to attain the deeper human person-hood that is so characteristic of authentic Personal-Spiritual Relationships. In this way, then, positive Personal-Spiritual Relationships evolve as Appreciate Human Activity Systems in which colleagues respect one another.

> As with many of the most important things in life, Personal-Spiritual Relationships are paradoxical: They generate many of our difficulties while concurrently resolving many of our difficulties

Personal-Spiritual Relationships (P-SR), unlike Manipulative or even Functional Relationships, leave colleagues with a deeper awareness of the full human experience and emotional vulnerabilities that experience suggests. These in-depth relationships enable people to become more deeply aware of themselves and other persons as unique, free, and historical individuals. Through the Personal-Spiritual Relationship, you come to know the other person as a person in an unconditional and absolute way. Here, the other person is not the means to your ends. Rather, that other person is the end of infinite value.

This level of insightful interaction within the L4EH relationship generates deeper insights about the meaning of life than we normally gain through other kinds of relationships. Naturally, this creates expectations about the performance of people who form L4EH workplace relationships. These expectations motivate people to produce many of our most significant challenges. Have you ever noticed that in Personal-Spiritual Relationships, the expectations we have of ourselves disappoint us the most? In fact, unless you are fixated at L1EH, disappointment with ourselves, and to a lesser extent other people, is the most significant source of emotional pain we suffer in life.

Transpersonal Nature of P-SR

By their very nature as person-to-person, or dialogic, Personal-Spiritual Relationships are highly inter-active. They mirror Functional Relationships in this respect, especially as the working alliance becomes ever more inter-active. Since relationships are about what goes on between people, hopefully to move a project forward, the Personal-Spiritual Relationship eventually becomes Transpersonal as they continue to deepen and expand. The emergence of Transpersonal Relationships signifies a milestone for the people within it because they have reached a more profound depth of social expression. Such relationships, when they exist, are extremely sensitive and can deepen beyond words.

As you see, the Personal-Spiritual Relationship consists of several dimensions. Unlike the more constrained Objective and Manipulative Relationships, well-tuned Personal-Spiritual Workplace Relationships focus on the growth and experience of everyone in the relationship. No one minimizes anyone. No one ignores anyone. No one uses and abuses anyone. While the relationships associated with L1EH are one-dimensional and always go wrong, Personal-Spiritual Relationships are multi-dimensional and rarely go wrong. When they become distorted, however, people have put in a lot of effort to get them back on the right track, the reliability path forward as we like to say in project management.

Distorted P-SRs

Personal-Spiritual Relationships (P-SR) occasionally go off course for several reasons:

- Developmental histories become distorted;

- People become fixated by reliving past history, or
- People revert to unhealthy roles in response to the problems of other people.

Rather than functioning as a process for human growth, distorted Personal-Spiritual Relationships become empty processes that lead people to form other relationships to obtain reparative opportunities.

Human development occurs in cycles of progression, rather than as a vertical process of bottom-up maturation. In P-SRs, people freely participate in their own evolutionary unfolding (growth) by providing self-guided direction to their own life designs. This is potent stuff. It means that people in P-SRs, those enabled by L4EH, are guided by deeper values, missions, and visions. T4EH encourages human beings to reach out and accept the nature of their own transpersonal capacities for living a profound existence in P-SR with other human beings who are themselves moving along similar paths. As there are several dimensions to relationships emerging from T4EH, the transcendent dimensions of meaning and creativity for example, multiple dimensions to the P-SR likewise exist.

As a human being, you are a relationship designer. You live well as you construct a Human Relationship Process Model that offers a behavioral capability that, when realized, enables you to balance your life. In practice, balance is the golden mean mentioned by Aristotle. Balance creates a developmental integrity that enables you to move to ever deeper and more profound experiences of life beginning in childhood and progressing to an age of advanced maturity. It is a values-laden life that frees the individual to become a person of integrity. It is integrity, then, that serves as the stairway to freedom.

P-SRs and Happiness

Have you noticed that nowhere do I say that T4EH is a hunger for happiness? I speak about growth and development. I speak about potency. I speak about creativity, fullness, and profound living, but nowhere do I mention happiness. I do not mention happiness for good reason. As a fairly happy and joyful person, I rarely think about happiness. In fact, I know enough about happiness that I avoid bringing up the topic with other people. Mostly unhappy people seek happiness as a life goal. They seek what they cannot find.

P-SRs are experienced as powerful emergent cycles of processes through which people enhance their emotional well-being. This is the responsibility of everyone, to enhance their own emotional well-being. Happiness is paradoxical: People have to find happiness for themselves, but as long as they look for it, they will never find it. Human beings cannot find happiness; they have to BE happy. As long as you look for it, as long as you seek it, you do not have it. Stop looking for it, and you will find it.

No one can give happiness to another because no one can ever have happiness. It is experienced in the non-seeking. You can never be happy by desiring happiness because you can only chase what you do not have. Happy people enjoy their happy state of being. They do not desire happiness while they are enjoying it. They do, however, make a decision to cultivate emotional peace in their lives and the lives of other people.

The Law for Being Happy: Do Not Chase Happiness

Authors of books about happiness actually have quite a bit of trouble describing happiness to people who want to be happy. Happiness comes forth when we look back on "happy times". Happy people do not stop to question their own happiness. Doing so would make one very unhappy. The more people talk about their happiness or write books about their happiness, or seek happiness, the more everyone else becomes unhappy. Who wants to be left out?

Unhappy people are not really unhappy. They are lonely for a substantial experience of life. Personal-Spiritual Relationships often provide this substantial experience. Human beings can never have happiness. It is not a possession. It is not about having. However, human beings can be happy. Happiness emerges from the process of becoming fully human, and it is engendered by peace and balance and overcoming the perennial disappointments of a fragile human life.

> The first rule in becoming fully human: Avoid those people who promise to make you happy. You are in trouble already.

This brings us to the end of Chapter Five. By now you should understand the impact that Existential Hunger has on the development of your workplace relationships and the kinds of relationships that emerge from the four levels of Existential Hunger. This natural hunger creates the background energy of human drama. In mastering your relationships, start with Existential Hunger. Next, consider the kinds of relationships that emerge from it. Remember that these first six chapters have introduced you to the levels of Existential Hunger forming a Human Relationships Process Model of Workplace Relationships.

Chapter Six continues to fill-in the Human Relationships Process Model (HRPM). Here we explore the place of rationality revealed in the HRPM of workplace relationships and its role in associating the Levels of Existential Hunger with the kinds of relationships people experience.

The HRPM facilitates problem-solving. Through the HRPM, the focus shifts from Continuous Performance Management to Insider Threat Prevention Cyber Security as a necessity for raising performance and from the manager to the team. This dual shift requires the organization to place ITPCS and CPM Unification on a business and performance basis and ensure that knowledge transfer is expansive rather than situational and long term rather than temporary. We cannot live a good life without Personal-Spiritual Relationships, but we certainly can live a bad life with them.

7: Complex Relationships

Welcome to Chapter Six. We have examined the link between the "core influencers of life" and their association with the formation of potent relationships at work. You now have a clearer idea of how you formed your relationships at work and what went into making them the relationships they ultimately became.

The first five chapters presented a potent framework for understanding the levels of Existential Hunger that drive human beings to form specific workplace relationships. Existential Hunger compels people to manage relationships in specific ways. This innate hunger influences all of our relationships in good and bad ways. The first six chapters explored the relationships that emerge at each level of Existential Hunger.

You may remember that I referred to the Existential Hunger framework as the "Human Relationship Process Model". You can use this Model to examine the relationships you have endured over the years. It enables you to more deeply understand the experiences you may have endured with your workmates, from boss to subordinate and friend to stranger.

I recommend that you master the power of the Human Relationship Process Model to improve your workplace performance. As you do, you will see that you are better prepared to design your future relationships as you guide their evolutionary unfolding. Once mastered, the Model enables you to better understand:

- the people in your relationships;
- their reactions to you, and
- how you can consistently improve your relationships.

I designed this Model to assist you in understanding the dynamics driving each of your relationships. The Model enables you to predict:

- how the people you encounter on the job will behave towards you and other people within your relationships, and
- how you may want to respond to them to enhance workplace

performance.

Moreover, this enables you to uncover the great mystery regarding the kind of person you have become in response to the Level of Existential Hunger that guides your experience. The Model reveals:

- why you enter the kinds of relationships you do, and
- what other people can expect of you.

Although the Model does all of this for you, it does not force you to care about your relationships. If you are the kind of person who seeks out and establishes Manipulative Relationships, you will not care much that you use and dispose of people as long as you get what you want from them. You little care that you experience colleagues as a means to your ends regardless of the cost to them.

There will likely come a time, however, when such L1EH relationships will not be satisfying at the deeper emotional level where people most intimately exist and want to connect. There will come a time when L2EH relationships will not be satisfying to your heart. There will come a time when L3EH relationships will make you question the lack of richness in your life and the hollowness of your existence. I can only hope that you learn to enjoy such movements before you have spent most of your life manipulating and objectifying your friends and colleagues. You see, the nagging questions remain: Should people enter into relationships with you? Are you really good for them?

Hopefully, a time will arrive when you want more out of life than merely obsessive fear and the emptiness of associating with other L1EH human beings. As your emotional life develops, you will want more out of life than this. When this time arrives, you will be ready to continue on to the next level of growth. When the stages of transition arrive, you should reflect on the Human Relationship Process Model outlined in this book. It will teach you about the missing parts in your own development as an ever-evolving human being and what to do about it.

The Human Relationship Process Model will guide you along the path of your evolutional unfolding. If you pay attention to the insight it presents, it will guide you on your way to becoming a fully capable human person, the quest of every one of us. What is that old commercial: "You can pay me now, or pay me later." Life is much like this: You can grow up now, or you can grow up later. Believe me, now is better. He who hesitates is lost. The question arises, however: Is the Model objectively real or is it simply a matter of faith? This, of course, is a very reasonable question that deserves a reasonable answer.

Embedded Relationship at Work

Thus far you have seen how Existential Hunger influences people to form the kinds of relationships they form. You have also seen how these relationships flow from each level of hunger. I have also designed the Human Relationship Process Model to better describe the workplace relationships you now know. The challenge now is to build more productive workplace relationships by using the Model where one level of Existential Hunger is associated with specific kinds of relationships. We can do this by considering the embedded and hybrid factors that characterize many organizations and their workplace relationships.

Embedded relationships exist when multiple types of Existential Hunger occur concurrently, as when a single relationship is influenced by every type of Existential Hunger to such an extent that a single classification fails. These are the embedded relationships. In Chapter Eight, we will consider the nature of these kinds of relationships by first considering the influence that faith and reason exert on their formation. Perennial conflict between faith and reason is never ending and intrudes into every corner of human experience. Indeed, the agitation of faith and reason influences the kinds of relationships that human beings experience throughout their professional careers, and beyond throughout even their lifetimes.

Continuum of Relationships

Relationships differ. Every relationship is different even from itself on a daily basis. While human beings may not be able to step into the same river twice, they certainly cannot enter the same relationship twice. As a system with human beings as components, relationships exist on a continuum from open to closed, complex to simple (restricted), unitary to pluralist, and mechanistic to systemic.

The Continuum of Relationships

Everyone has good and bad days. On a good day, it is easy to be generous and considerate of other people. On a bad day, however, everything becomes difficult. On such days, people prefer to think about themselves more than other people as Level One Existential Hunger raises its ugly head. Even saints occasionally forget about other people. Growth to higher levels of Existential Hunger does not mean that a person has reached that level of Existential Hunger completely with no influences from the tugs of the heart that arise from previous levels of Existential Hunger.

Human beings are complex and dynamic beings. History occurs inside us as we move from one level of Existential Hunger to the next and sometimes back again. Psychologists refer to this as transference and counter-transference. "We live, breath, and have our being" as a people in flux moving forever forward. Time and need are variables in the dynamics of human growth. While time and need are the two forces that set the cycle of human nature into motion, faith and reason are the forces that lead us through the Continuum of Relationships and enable us to experience the joys and sorrows of emotional growth.

Faith and Reason in Relationships at Work

Faith and reason complicate everything. People are indeed complex beings. Our knowledge is finite, but our ignorance is infinite. People commonly advocate values they do not internalize and cannot ever internalize if the people are left to themselves. People commonly choose to ignore facts that will simplify their lives. Simply put: Broken and fractured workplace relationships are not accidental.

People see the speck in their neighbor's eyes but miss the log in their own. Yet we go to the moon and back. We land on Mars and count the stars. We explore beyond the solar system, while still in our scientific infancy. We transplant hearts and lungs, but remain stumped by the common cold. We do brain surgery but cannot build environmentally friendly automobile engines.

Occasionally, we love one another very deeply "beyond words," but ignore the meaning such love brings to the substance of our souls. Yet we seek the approval of even strangers as if that approval will define the worth of our existence. Through all of this, we remain incomplete because we owe our very existence to something much greater than ourselves. We are not the cause of our being, nor the cause of our existence. We are participators in our great experience of life, but not our originators of it.

All around us we stand at the edge of nothingness, but find our substance in the love of life. Love gives meaning to our lives and marks our uniqueness in all the cosmos regardless of our incapacity to create or even adequately understand and explain ourselves. Yet it is reasonable to fear ourselves for the history of our species disturbs peaceful sleep. Our history, after all, is the legacy of the kinds of relationships we experience.

> A grand mystery stands always before us: Hope, trust, and reason transform us into cosmologically wonderful beings, with all the potential of navigating the ever-evolving universe.

Trustworthy people trust people. Hopeful people hope. In workplace relationships, such people bring these perennial virtues into their environments. Manipulative people leverage such virtue against the trusting and hopeful others, but only for a while. Then reason does its work and dispels all myth of togetherness, especially the myth that obscures the true nature of L1EH workplace relationships. Faith and Reason (F&R) give rise to many questions.

Complicating Questions

The challenge for us now in examining workplace relationships is to clearly articulate the role that faith and reason play in human relationships. For example, what is reason and in what way do people behave rationality in workplace relationships? When we say that human beings are rational creatures, are we saying that human beings are rational in the same way in the same relationship at the same time? Does faith work the same way in every relationship and even with the same person? Is reason superior to faith?

If rationality is a particularly human way of understanding the world, is faith a particularly human way of remaining ignorant of the world? Or, does reason negate faith? Can one person encounter the world with a highly developed rational perspective and still be dominated by faith when making the most vital decisions of life? Are people more rational when they experience the relationships associated with L3EH or were they more rational during the L1EH phase? Is rational behavior the same regardless of Existential Hunger type or relationship experienced? We are met with many far-reaching questions, right?

Reason is reason and faith is faith, they contradict each other, right? Is it fair to say that persons imbued with deep faith are rationally immature? Is it fair to say that extreme examples of religious faith demonstrate the common sentiment that where faith dwells reason takes a holiday? Are such questions an indicator of the battle between faith and reason? Are we humans so simplistic that whenever we abandon reason to faith we become less than what we could be? What is faith?

Chapter Seven will address these questions and integrate them into the Human Relationship Process Model. You will see that this Model consists not only of the different Levels of Existential Hunger and the relationships associated with them, but includes further considerations of Fideism and Rationality, the complicating factors that produce the complexity of organization life. Beyond this, we also discuss more deeply the Continuum of Human Relationships.

The application of the Human Relationships Process Model is skills based and testifies to proficiencies in the behavioral skills, sciences, and core competencies necessary to attain success in the modern workplace. You can employ the HRPM to solve problems of relationship development and assist with the professional preparation of Cyber Security success. We designed the HRPM to assist executives, information technology professionals, and those in the middle who engage in the activities of Insider Threat Prevention Cyber Security to facilitate the success of an organization's enterprise strategies.

Relationships begin in the confluence where hope meets trust. Relationships change in the experience where reason dispels all projections.

8: Rational Side of Relationships

Welcome to Chapter Eight. Previously, we examined the levels of Existential Hunger, kinds of relationships, the core influencers of life such as virtues and behaviors, the Human Relationship Process Model, faith and reason, and the relevance of all of this to relationships in organizations. If you have digested the last several chapters, and have managed to overcome the tendency to disregard free advice, you will have gained insight into the nature of the relationships you form with colleagues, friends, and family.

I organized this book to assist you with mastering the finer points that govern your workplace relationships. As a bonus, you should better understand your relationships with family and friends. As you master this book, you will find that it was worth the effort. Do yourself a favor and reduce your propensity for sliding by; many people have such a propensity. Be smart and use this book to build potent relationships. It is the rational thing to do. There is that word again, rational.

Faith and Reason in Workplace Relationships

We have come to the point where we can explore the roles of faith and reason in experiencing relationships. The previous chapter made the case that the conflict between faith and reason complicates our experience of organizations. This is because we often see things that are not there and miss the things that are there. Even with a finely tuned mind that has developed the powerful capacity for reasoning well, human beings short-change themselves way too often by filtering everything through the lens of selective emotional perception and hyper-focused intellectualization (not a medical condition).

Chapter Seven asked a boatload of questions about faith and reason. How well did you do with them? Did you chance upon some thought-provoking answers? If so, you belong to a rare group of thinkers. Seriously, though, questions regarding the conflict between faith and reason have challenged humanity since before the Enlightenment. The conflict between faith and reason has led many a brave soul into cognitive ruin. No doubt you have heard a story or two about some poor philosopher who took up basket weaving to save what was left of his mind.

The problem of faith versus reason has the potential to scramble eggs. It remains a hot conflict. If you are careful to clarify your terms before engaging the enemy, you will be alright. Faith is faith and reason is reason. Right? Well, not really. I may believe that I have the gift of reason, but I cannot prove it as easily, if at all. Saying it is so is easy, but proving that it is so takes a bunch of work. However, I believe that we can do the work because I believe that we are rational people. After all, we are reasonable if nothing else, I believe. This is what I believe, although I cannot prove it rationally. I do know that I am rational because I believe it. Get the point?

Impact of Faith on Workplace Relationships

Human Reasoning is a particularly mindful process that most often employs specific rules of investigation to gain knowledge about a particular domain of human experience. Generally, reasoning delivers knowledge that is gained whenever human beings use their intellects in the right way, the reasonable way.

Disciplined reasoning, or Rationalism, offers an approach to knowledge gathering that differs considerably from the pronouncements of mere commonplace opinion which may or may not be truthful. Although a few scientists prefer the search for facts, knowledge gained through reasoning concerns the search for truth. People view such truth-driven reasoning as rational whenever it meets, at a minimum, the following four criteria. Reasoning:

- Includes appropriate justifications.
- Offers pertinent reasons for affirmation.
- Delivers accepted factual evidence.
- Offers verification using knowledge derived from sensory experience and external awareness of perceived conditions.

Opinion most often expresses belief while rationalism seeks truth. Occasionally opinion and rationalism proclaim the same truth and same falsehood.

Relationships of every kind frequently share opinions about nearly everything. This is because every relationship is energized by an act of faith termed trust. Within your workplace relationships, you implicitly trust yourself to do what you should do. You also trust colleagues to conduct their affairs in an expected manner. For example, people in relationships place their trust in their relationships, at least somewhat. They especially have faith in the relationships they enjoy and little trust in the ones they do not enjoy. They believe in their relationships if they feel good about them. Of course, people remain loyal for years to the people they feel good about.

Relationships make demands on us that impact our social existence. Some people experience relationships as an extension of their lives of faith. These people experience the world, relationships, and their approach to rationality, indeed their entire lives, as constitutive elements of their lives of faith. Some of these people may even embed rationality within the context of a living faith. For these people, faith is the structure in which reason operates. Philosophers refer to this position as Fideism. Here faith is a priori to reasoning: We believe that we can know truth. Do you believe it?

Submissive Workmates

If you open your mind's eye, you can see how Fideism impacts your experience of relationships. People who engage the world through Fideism are fundamentally submissive to authority. They respect the rules and regulations that define the relationship and govern its conduct. Managers love these people because they do what they are told without question. Since they operate from a position that demands linguistic understanding, they respect the authority expressed in the written guidelines of management. You can expect such people to actively avoid the exercise of reasoning whenever possible. Entire cultures can function like this. When societies, or organization, make the wrong turn, committed fideist can become committed terrorists.

When you encounter people like this in your workplace relationships, you can expect them to accept the commands of superiors without question. If you are a manager or a teammate in a L2EH relationship or above, this is a double-edged sword. Professional relationships require independent judgment, never blind faith. However, managers of L1EH relationships love these people because they are pliable targets of manipulation.

Think about this for a moment. In what kinds of relationships would you expect such people to prosper? What type of Existential Hunger do you think defines them? How do they relate to colleagues? People following this perspective of faith ignore rational or scientific explanations for the actions of organizations and relationships. They are often indifferent to rational thought and prefer to receive everything in writing.

Faith of Superior Understanding

All kinds of people form relationships and bond with each other. Some of them hold many opinions and believe that they have attained an in-depth understanding of some of the most central secrets of life. Although it is true that everyone knows something, it is also true that everyone knows less than they believe. In fact, it is faith in their beliefs that leads many people to believe that they have a higher understanding of truth than is possible with reason alone. For these people, faith is far superior to rationality when it comes to understanding life's most sublime mysteries.

When you work with people like these, some interesting things can happen. You will discover that such people are bigger than themselves. They commit themselves to the immediate tasks and activities before them. They focus more on the needs of other people in their relationships, and take care of their own needs last. These people create a strong impression of richness in attitude. They see things very profoundly and are understood at the higher levels of the organization better than they are at the lower levels.

Most people simply do not understand these people very well and are bothered by the convictions they bring to the job. They believe in themselves, and they believe in you just as strongly. While very rational people tend towards individuality, pursue self-seeking goals, and often fail to see the fullness of human life, people of faith often see the profound nature of human experience.

Faith Clarifies Understanding

Some people experience relationships as if they were religious encounters. For these people, faith orders and expands human reasoning. Differing from Fideism, religious faith can open access to extra dimensions in life that are ordinarily missed by less faith-filled individuals. When properly balanced in the work environment, these people strive to be fair and stress the equality of workmates. You can expect good things from the people who bring this kind of perspective to your workplace relationships. They will be sensitive, fair, insightful, and modest. They will never bore you to tears by responding to any situation with exaggerated rationalizations.

Faith Overcomes Reason

Occasionally workplace relationships involve people who maintain that faith is the foundation of all truth. Unlike some people in the management ranks, faith-based people maintain that faith is more certain than reason. They argue that rules of reason and scientific formulations are not necessarily certain. Even the generally accepted principles of science can be incorrect as later discoveries reveal new truths found in new evidence.

You can expect to relax around people who are driven by their faith in this direction. They are confident, relaxed, truthful, and calm people. They contribute to relationships by exerting a positive influence during difficult situations. They are very good at reducing the negative impact of the more rational individuals who now and then view themselves as superior human beings. Such arrogance is easily overcome by the humility of these faith-filled team members. Obviously, the record of pure rational behavior is mixed.

Relationships consisting of purely rational people exhibit a range of issues uncommon among faith-filled relationships. For example, purely rational people are often unable to see the truth of inter-personal situations. They are known to actually hate people who appear different from themselves, and can become oppressively unjust and unreliable. On the other hand, relationships involving rational and faith-filled people are complex, but very creative.

Non-Reductionist Perspectives

Rationalism reduces human understanding to elemental components of knowledge. This has a special place in science and engineering, but not necessarily in relationships. Some people advocate a faith-filled life that opens their relationships to the richness and complexity of the expansiveness of human life. Non-reductionist, faith-filled relationships enable people to overcome the constraints of the exaggerated reductionism of over rationalization common among many organizations within high-tech companies. Because they can be creative, people with this faith-filled perspective excel as designers and systems thinkers.

Balanced-Life Perspectives

Human beings are creatures of faith and reason. Understanding that reason has its limits, people with a deeply held and lived-faith have the courage to take risks, and explore unchartered territory. They are "go beyond" people who do not settle for the ordinary and comfortable situations in life. They go beyond their rational grounding to connect with the potential of their infinite life.

These people are possibility thinkers who are never quite comfortable with the status quo. This attitude expands the capabilities of the relationships they join. Not ignorant of the potency of reason in the discovery and solutions of human problems, these people face life with an attitude that accommodates both reason and faith. Being creatures of faith, however, they remain keenly aware of the fallible nature of cause-and-effect explanations about life.

Trustfulness in Perspective

Some people participate in relationships guided by their trust in a life bigger than themselves. These people live visions that invite other people to share their lives. They understand that independence is never complete and that every human being is fulfilled in experiencing positive relationships with their families, friends, teachers, workmates, leaders, and even enemies. In the workplace, these people understand that their decisions are not only their own but may impact everyone in the organization.

Understanding that other people can enrich their own lives, they want to be trusted and respond to other people with trust. They act in a way that communicates their acceptance of people in their relationships. When you work with such people, you soon discover that they are powerful individuals who confidently bring their values and meaning to their relationships and the larger organization. In accepting them in your organization, you gain the inspiration of their faith and the encouragement to see the organization as something more significant than an environment governed by a few rational principles. Such people are inspiring. They likewise find their inspiration in the relationships they experience.

Faith Beyond Reason Perspective

Some people in relationships believe that faith and reason are separate powers of human beings. However, these people see faith as superior to reason and well beyond reason in its power to support human existence. For them, it is more faith than reason that makes our species human. In the workplace, these people can be difficult to get along with because they place their beliefs, religious or otherwise, above the beliefs of everyone else, and even above the rational processes common to organization life.

If you do not share their beliefs, whatever they are, you are an outsider. You will never be able to reach them by making an appeal to reason. You have to become an insider, one of them, sharing their beliefs. Or, in their eyes, you just cannot get it. They expect you to walk in their shoes for some time to be one of them. Then, and only then, can you experience the kind of relationships that can be fully productive.

When such a person works for you, you will soon discover that this person may not accept your evaluation of his (or her) performance because you are using an externally rational approach. You are an outsider, and that is that. People who commit to a faith without reason connect at a deep level only with those who share their beliefs, whatever they are, casual or radical.

Place of Faith in Relationships

Sometimes knowledge is not enough, especially when we realize that reason is fallible. At such times, we have to trust the rational powers of other human beings. We do not know if their reasoning process is flawed. There is no escaping the hold of faith on the life of every human being. We even have to believe in the truth of our rational processes. They seem to work; they seem to be practical, and they seem to make sense. Inevitably, however, they break down. When this occurs, we re-energize rationality through new learning and our belief in the efficacy of our capacity for knowing truth, the most fundamental belief of every rational person. I cannot prove that any of us have the ability to know the truth of anything. I can only assert it by appealing to faith in our capacity to know truth, the fundamental presupposition of human existence.

Some kinds of relationships demand more faith than other kinds of relationships. Think about your own experience. Do Manipulative Relationships tax your faith the most? Or do Personal Relationships lead you to believe in other people the most? What type of Existential Hunger requires more faith than reason? Is faith directly or inversely proportional to the type of Existential Hunger one is experiencing and thus the kind of workplace relationships one forms? Are you beginning to see the power of the Human Relationship Process Model in resolving such dilemmas? Obviously, faith plays a role in your experience of relationships. What about reason?

Occasionally, opinion is not enough to do the work demanded in maintaining effective relationships. Whether or not we like it, certain situations demand that human beings exercise their power of reason, a painful responsibility for many people no doubt. For example, such a demand occurs whenever a specialized kind of knowledge is required to advance the agenda of the relationship, like improving the durability of the materials used in space flight.

Astronauts have a lot of faith, no doubt, but they use highly refined empirical science to keep them safe when going to the moon. They have faith in empirical science. So let us move now from our discussion about the impact of faith on relationships to explore the other side of the coin, human reason and its role in maintaining relationships.

Logical Reasoning Perspective

Relationships also involve rational people who like to think things out before attempting a task. They are very logical and like to move from premises to logical conclusions. They are most content when the people around them take the same approach. Human beings possess the capacity to act logically, after all. Therefore, you must rigorously follow the rules of logic, even when you do not know what these rules mean, what they are, or how they work.

Rationality Identity

In a similar manner, but without the logical processes of disciplined inquiry, workplace relationships often involve people who "believe" that everyone must think and act rationally. There are no exceptions to the rule. The only way to be human is to be rational. Such things as faith, religion, and belief are for the fearful who need something to hold themselves together because life is too challenging. This is what the people with "Rationality Identity" bring to their relationships, their "belief" in the power and capacity of human beings to be rational in every situation. It is, after all, their "belief" that Rationality Identity is the defining mark of human nature. Welcome to the Western Worldview of human nature.

In corporate life, special kinds of organizations consist of an abundance of people who maintain this perspective about human nature: We are the rational animal. In the right environments, such people can be quite successful in areas that require in-depth analysis and synthesis. In management areas, however, they can be tough on their workmates who relate to the world from a lived-faith perspective. When these people have to work with individuals who maintain that faith is the defining and superior power of human nature, the one that defines us as a species, the dialogues can become very heated. Nevertheless, such relationship combat remains a low-level form of entertainment for those external to the relationship.

Reason is Understanding Perspective

Some people go beyond the rational perspectives mentioned above by stipulating that efforts in reason are only rational if the end goal is understanding rather than merely the attainment of knowledge. These people are more profound than most other people involved in organization relationships. They have attained the insight that "understanding" is worth its extra effort in platinum. Today, we understand that the capacity for high-level abstract thinking, that is, thinking about "First Principles" and "Ultimate Causes", is a universal indicator of human intelligence. As far back as the 13th Century, Thomas Aquinas had already recognized this truth.

> "Experience shows that some understand more profoundly than do others; as one who carries a conclusion to its first principles and ultimate causes understands it better than one who reduces it to its proximate causes." (Thomas Aquinas, Summa Theologica, I,Q. 85, art 7.)

Authentic human progress occurs sporadically. Such unique progress takes form whenever knowledge moves from the simple perception of facts and data, the proximate causes, to the transformation of human experience, first principles and ultimate causes, through which the knower becomes a substantially wiser person. While knowledge results from simple loop learning, wisdom begins to emerge with the advent of double and triple loop learning.

Learning like this is rare and requires the desire and effort to be wise, to really understand the world we inhabit, shape, destroy, and enjoy. This intellectual and emotional experience is authentic Mindfulness.

If you take your intellect seriously, and many people are reluctant to think about their intellects, working with people like these can become a genuine pleasure. You will learn many things about everything that you probably never thought about before, from Astronomy to Zoology. The problem with people who continually search for understanding is that they might not want to understand the things they need to understand to make the workplace relationship successful. There will come a time when your agenda definitely will not be their agenda. This often ignites disagreements, gets processes off track, and sets some people back in their goals.

People can be distracted by other people who continually seek understanding in everything they do. As a manager, you would be wise to learn how to encourage these people to stay the course and become part of the solution rather than become only another problem. Smart managers know how to lead them to "understand" their value to the relationship. Smart managers know how to encourage them to use their great gifts for the good of the organization.

Fideism Rationality

Some people employ reason to overcome particular objections to their belief systems. Relationships with these people become intriguing. Not only do they advocate the supremacy of faith over reason but they employ reasoning to make sense of the reasoning that justified the elevation of faith. They advocate a lived-faith but only for reasons that make logical sense. These people, therefore, apply reason to resolve any doubts that may impede the free exercise of their faith. In this way, their faith becomes a reasonable faith that everyone can adopt. You can count on these people to be committed to their lived-faith but for rational reasons rather than emotional ones. Their belief system is important but only insofar as it can be shown to be reasonable. If you have people like these in your organization, you will find that they are not gullible. They work in a deliberate manner. They will be very loyal if such loyalty can be shown to make sense. If you are a manager, you can motivate these people by providing a sound rationale for your requests. They may have faith in you, but only if you can provide a good reason for them to believe in you.

Rationality In-Service of Fideism

Some people use reason to deepen their faith and expand its reach into a wider area of experience. Basically, they employ reason to deepen their lived-faith by increasing the understanding of the dimensions of faith in general and their faith specifically. For them, therefore, reason becomes the mechanism that enables them to experience an ever-developing belief system.

Involving people like these in your relationships is notable for several reasons. First, they will continually attempt to master and develop their workplace relationships. They are considerate and like to keep their commitments. You will find that such people operate best in a relationship that is associated with Level Three Existential Hunger. They are not high ego state, or manipulative, but enjoy reaching out to other people and contributing to the goals of an organization. Considering their desire for self-development, their attitude towards growth and performance makes sense.

Conceptual World Rationality

Workplace relationships that involve these conceptual kinds of people are quite logical. These individuals easily master the conceptual models that lead to deeper insights of the intellect. They build grand systems of thought in which faith is one of the many possible components of human experience. Faith is known rationally. It has its place in human experience, but it is only one aspect of that experience. Although the workplace relationship can justify faith, and even admit that it may make sense in the larger scheme of things, nevertheless, it places little more emphasis on faith than this. Conceptually rational people may even question the reasonableness of a p[articular faith system and see it as irrational. Human reason is the criteria for the reasonableness found within the framework of any faith experience.

Working with individuals like these is like being a member of a special kind of think tank. However, if you are not this kind of thinker, but work in an environment like this, you may imagine that you are on the planet Vulcan. If you are a person of faith, these people will respect you, admit you to their company, but rationalize your beliefs as nothing more than a single aspect of the organization's reservoir of conceptual awareness. In their eyes, your beliefs earn no particular prominence, and may even appear to you to be under-valued. Your faith system will be viewed as a single component of the Spiritual Capital that you bring to the relationship.

Superior Rationality

Related to the "grand scheme of things" type of person discussed above, there are people who only accept a faith explained in rational terms. Although this appears contradictory, these people argue that one cannot have an actual faith, if that faith cannot be explained rationally. Otherwise, people practice an irrational faith and are victims of a delusion. In this view, even God must be explained rationally. For these people, human life contains no mystery.

If God exists, God can be known completely through the proper exercise of human reason. Indeed, these individuals argue that human beings betray their own essential natures whenever they accept some sort of supernatural or religious mystery as being beyond human explanation. Reason is superior to faith they maintain. Therefore. every believer must be capable of explaining every religious belief he or she holds.

People with this view of human existence tend to be less open or imaginative than other people who are less stuck on the prominence of rationalism in human experience. However, they are well-grounded individuals who expect solid proof to all claims of mystery, regardless of where the claim originated, whether in faith or even in the practical affairs of business, politics, management, or science. For these people, workplace relationships have to make sense, especially if they are to remain committed to the success of any Insider Threat Prevention Cyber Security program.

Fideistic Rationality

We have now arrived at the final personality state from the Human Relationship Process Model that I wish to discuss. These people enjoy a perspective of rationality that is empirical. However, this empiricism flows from a faith perspective that is grounded in experience rather than on the measurement of a material category. These individuals are the great observers who do not put everything in logical categories. Rather, they describe the processes, inputs, outputs, and transformations of human experience to deepen their understanding of their faith, or their lived human experience, as transformational.

These individuals do not engage in empirical science as a goal-driven discipline. Rather, they experience rationality guided by faith in general as a way of living. These people use faith to guide them as a general principle of human experience. Their perspective, therefore, is experienced as a way of life. It is lived out by examination, continual questioning, and description, rather than as a method of empirical measurement. They are the relationship phenomenologists of human experience.

These people produce the descriptions of the experiences of human life, including the experience of faith as something evolving and always in a state of becoming. One might say that they see human experience as continually “in-flux”. Since they realize that they experience the world through their physical senses, they possess a keen “point-of-view” about the types of knowledge we human beings are capable of enjoying. They understand the range of reason and the limits of understanding. So they do not deny what people experience, whatever it may be. Rather they describe the experience of faith as seriously as they describe the experience of engineering because faith like engineering is experienced.

This perspective was very prominent among the theologians, philosophers, psychologists, and phenomenological thinkers of the 20th Century, as well as a select group of empiricists of the 19th Century. One may say that these individuals are not so much committed to the search for knowledge as an ultimate goal of life. Rather, they are involved in the quest of understanding the world of human phenomena. Moreover, they seek to understand the experience of humanity as a lived experience, not merely as rational approach of rational human beings seeking ultimate understanding. They describe themselves fundamentally as people of faith seeking understanding.

Rationalists would never choose to describe themselves this way. Unlike some of the other people floating around in organizations today, people who view the world this way may make perfect colleagues. They make open, inclusive, non-divisive, full of wonder, growth oriented, and curious colleagues. Historically, such people contributed to the development of the great mother of the empirical sciences, Physics. This science investigates the domains of experience that cannot be investigated solely with the physical senses, but requires faith and reason. Faith, so it seems, influences every aspect of human existence including science and reason.

Today, Fideistic Rationality is maturing more rapidly than at any time since its emergence. People employ a Fideistic Rationality to understand their experiences, whether at home, at work, or even in religion. The best thinkers from this school would say that Fideistic Rationality (my term) does not exist to eliminate or counter faith in the world. Rather it exists to discover the richness of human experience. Fidiestic Rationality is faith seeking understanding. This argument departs from the thinking of people who hold a faith based on some fundamental linguistic experience that restricts human reason even from questioning the meaning of their own lived and experienced faith.

Here is a question for you: Based on the Human Relationship Process Model, what do you think a workplace relationship would be like with people like this? What level of Existential Hunger would you say influences them? What Kind of relationship do you think they would enjoy? What kind of values do you believe they would advocate and virtues they would practice? What kind of Human Activity System is best suited to these kinds of people? Are they persons of virtue?

This last question is indeed a trick question. Here are a few more: What is a Human Activity System? How many types of Human Activity Systems are there? What is the difference between Human Activity Systems and other kinds of systems? Are Human Activity Systems real or are they only conceptual models?

The questions about Human Activity Systems are vital to mastering the Human Relationship Process Model. Existential Hunger, relationship type, and Human Activity Systems (HAS) form the three pillars of potent relationships at work. Previously we examined Existential Hunger and relationship type. In Chapter Eight, we begin our examination of Human Activity Systems as a design model for describing potent Unified ITPCS and CPM workplace relationships.

Relationships begin in the confluence where hope meets trust. Relationships change in the experience where reason dispels all projections.

9: Designing Potent Relationships

Welcome to Chapter Nine. Here we move from Existential Hunger and the associated kind of workplace relationships to the design CPM and ITPCS Human Activity Systems. This third component in the design of potent workplace relationships wraps everything up. Thanks to a singular question of my esteemed colleague at the Systems Management Institute, I have constructed a powerful framework to assist you with more effectively managing your workplace relationships.

The problem with concepts, of course, is that people become confused when they talk about them. This is because concepts are often much more than merely concepts. Occasionally, concepts describe real stuff out there in the world of our experience. For example, models of Human Activity Systems are powerful images used to describe actual Human Activity Systems (HAS). These are systems in which human beings are the components.

Here is something else to think about, but it may be a bit obscure: Psychologists claim that people project all the time. They say this because people do project a lot. That people project is a psychological concept of human behavior. The human behavior involved is indeed projection. You project for your own reasons, defensive reasons. The concept and the behavior are the same. This brings up our first interesting point about Human Activity Systems: A system is what a system does.

A System is What a System Does

Many years ago, a student and I had dinner in a senior care home. While we were busy discussing the fate of the world, we happened to glance at two people nearby. I observed that one of them was actively engaged in the psychological behavior of projection. When the student witnessed what had taken place, he exclaimed: "Gosh, look at that guy over there. He is projecting. Wow projection does occur. I thought it was all psychobabble."

Projection is not only a psychological concept. Projection is a term that describes what people do when they project. The reason they project is another discussion and not the issue here. The point for us here is that concepts are often more than concepts. They are real experiences that we understand, describe, and name. We simply use concepts to describe what is. "It is what it is. It is what it does." Have you ever noticed that wherever you are, that is where you are? Now this is an important concept.

Let me repeat, Human Activity Systems are systems in which the principal components are human beings. Human beings do form systems in which they transform some kind of matter, energy, or information inputs into some kind of matter, energy, and information outputs. This is not merely a concept. The HAS model describes a real experience of human beings organized in a particular way to act in a particular way within specific relationships to produce outcomes.

Workplace Relationships exist. Organizations embedded with workplace relationships exist. Many times, relationships exist in organizations to transform inputs into outputs. These few statements are statements of facts that have a reference to reality. The words we use to present the facts do not alter the facts whenever the facts that as stated enjoy a one-to-one correspondence with reality in such a way that mirrors and describes the facts as they genuinely exist in reality. Got it?

By the way, the process of correspondence provides a path for establishing a common definition of truth to the extent that we can unequivocally state: Truth exists whenever a conceptual fact in the mind corresponds with what is real in external reality as it exists at the time the correspondence exists. It is true that water is H2O conceptually only if water exists in reality as H2O in correspondence to the act of rendering the definition. For, it is possible for a correspondence between a conceptual being and real being to be transitory and impermanent. Timing of the correspondence matters.

A thing is whatever it is in reality. A system is what a system does. A Human Activity Systems is what a Human Activity System does. These are all concepts that are more than mere concepts. They are descriptions of reality and how we experience that reality as we live that reality. It is worth remembering that concepts are lived experiences of human beings.

Later we will put all the components in their proper place to finalize the Human Relationship Process Model. You will see then that the Model consists not only of levels of Existential Hunger, the associated relationships, and types of Human Activity Systems. It also includes the mix of personalities experiencing the relationships with their associated values, virtues, and passions such as rationalism and fideism.

This last consideration completes the final Human Relationship Process Model as a model for navigating sociopaths at work. We will now integrate the components of the Model to provide a working model to guide you through the tarpits and pitfalls of your career and assist you in navigating sociopaths at work as you unify Insider Threat Prevention Cyber Security and Continuous Performance Management.

Human Relationship Process Model

Welcome to the final sections of our examination of the levels of Existential Hunger and their associated relationships. We have journeyed across a vast and deep landscape and retroactively developed a map of the untamed territory of workplace relationships as if we were explorers entering a new but ancient land, the land of workplace relationships as Human Activity Systems.

In the remainder of this book, I will map out what we have uncovered so that you can employ this map to guide you along your own journey to a good life, whether in the workplace, at home, with strangers, or among your friends. The dynamics of all relationships are the same, they differ by social focus. We will begin this section with a summary of the Human Relationship Process Model so far. The Newkirk Human Relationship Process Model consists of several kinds of Existential Hunger within six Dimensions of experience. These include:

- Ego-Centric Existential Hunger
- Goal-Centered Existential Hunger
- Transcendental Existential Hunger, and
- Spiritual Existential Hunger

Dimension One: The Four Types of Existential Hunger, Levels One & Two
Dimension Two: Core Influencers of Life
Dimension Three: Values, Level One, and Value Clusters
Dimension Four: Five Types of Human Activity Systems
Dimension Five: Systems Continua
Dimension Six: Map of Systems Types

Type One Existential Hunger is Ego Centric Hunger consisting of Objective, Manipulative, and Deceitful Relationships.

Type Two Existential Hunger is Goal Centric Hunger consisting of Functional, Project Specific, and Teaming Relationships

Type Three Existential Hunger is Transcendent Hunger consisting of Personal, Empathetic, and Loving Relationships.

Type Four Existential Hunger is Spiritual Hunger consisting of Spiritual-Religious, Self-Guided Evolutionary, and Transformation Relationships.

Within Dimension Two, the Four Types of Existential Hunger at Level Two include the Core Influencers of Life consisting of Reason, Faith, Ethics, Morals, Values

Within Dimension Three we have Values at Level One consisting of our Values Clusters consisting of Self-Development, Relationship, Mastery, Social-Responsibility, Lifestyle, Continuity

Within Dimension Three we have Values, Level One consisting of Values Clusters, Instrumental Values, Aligned Values, Essence Specific Values, Extrinsic Values

Also, within Dimension Three we have Values, Level One, Value Clusters consisting of Self-Development, Relationship, Mastery, Social-Responsibility, Life-Style, and Continuity.

Dimension Four we have Five Types of Human Activity Systems consisting of Rigidly Controlled, Deterministic, Purposive, Hueristic, and Purpose Seeking.

Dimension Five we have the Systems Continua consisting of the Mechanistic to Systemic, Unitary to Pluralist, Restricted to Complex, and Closed to Open.

Dimension Six we have the Map of System Types consisting of the Closed to Mechanistic to Unitary to Restricted and from Open to Systemic to Pluralist to

Complex.

Summary: The Newkirk Human Relationship Process Model

Dimension One: The Four Types of Existential Hunger, Level One

Dimension One: The Four Types of Existential Hunger, Level Two

Dimension Two: Core Influencers of Life

Dimension Three: Values, Level One

Dimension Three: Values, Level One, Value Clusters

Dimension Four: Five Types of Human Activity Systems

Dimension Five: Systems Continua

Dimension Six: Map of Systems Types

Describing Relationships at Work

The first step in describing a relationship as a Human Activity System (HAS) is to recognize that people have a vested interest in their relationships. The impact of this awareness leads a person to think more deeply about the nature of the relationship. Several questions arise that profoundly influence our understanding of the nature of our workplace relationships. For example, what is a Human Activity System and how can one appropriately describe the relationship as a Human Activity System? What does it mean to describe our relationship as Human Activity System? What method do we use to craft this description? Lucky for us, the answers to these questions are surprisingly simple, as are the questions.

Simplicity is Potent

Human Activity Systems are living systems composed of human beings. A system consists of subsystems, components, processes and environments through which systems transform inputs into outputs. The inputs are matter, energy, and information. A system exists within an environment. The inputs come from the environment. The transformed outputs return to the environment. Fundamentally, that's it.

The selection of a method of system description is directly related to the purpose of the description. The effort of stating a purpose for the required description demands commitment. Commitment is the second step in describing our workplace relationship. Through the process of commitment, we can answer the question: Why study this relationship?

Following the awareness and commitment stage, we determine whether our relationship is indeed a Human Activity System. Does our relationship engage in transformation? If not, it is not a Human Activity System. To make such a determination, the observer applies the definition of systems to the defined activity. In this way, this third stage in describing our relationship is termed the detection stage. Can we detect any transformations within our relationship? We may hope so.

If we find that our relationship is indeed a Human Activity System, we examine the relationship to identify systems boundaries that separate subsystems and the environment. This is the separation stage; it defines the boundaries. At this point, we may decide to examine a single subsystem of our relationship based on the intent of the study. Here we may develop a root definition of the part of the relationship we are examining. This stage in the process of providing a description of the relationship is termed the selection stage. Here, we are concerned with the process of systems summarization through system identification.

As the sixth and final stage of formal systems description, we make useful models of the selected system. This stage, termed the description stage, requires at least six activities:

The System Description Stage

1. Define system's components.
2. Build environmental model which identifies all of the environmental components affecting the relationship.
3. Identify all inputs to and all outputs from the relationship.
4. Construct a process model of the relationship which identifies all of the state variables of the relationship.
5. Identify all of the relationships existing between the state variables of the process model, the infrastructure model.
6. Construct a structured model of the selected system which identifies all of the structural relationships between components.

The preceding descriptions are essential when modelling the selected relationship as a Human Activity System or its subsystems. Here we bring together the possible views about our relationship. We also continue to provide a problem solution, whatever the problem may be. The process of describing relationships is not linear. Frequently, we return to an earlier stage to obtain additional clarification and pursue further study. In the strictest sense, the method of describing relationships consists of iterative cycles of work.

This takes us to Part Three where we move from the discussion of technical systems design into the serious challenge of morals and ethics at work. As we examine the new digital environment of the 21st Century enterprise, we will also discuss the role of virtues in ensuring human freedom in the workplace now challenged by Cyber Terror.

Conclusion to Part Two

Part One explored the Psychology of Insider Threat Prevention Cyber Terror by examining the impact of sociopathology on workplace relationships and the risk of malicious insiders. While introducing the Hallmarks of Continuous Performance Management (CPM), the author questioned Continuous Performance Management's resiliency in the face of the threat of Cyber Terror. It argued that Continuous Performance Management and Cyber Terror are both psychological phenomena coming from opposite ends of the behavioral spectrum.

Part Two in the series continued the theme of Continuous Performance Management-Insider Threat Prevention Cyber Security Unification by introducing the Newkirk Human Relationship Process Model as it begins to form the ITP Cyber Security strategies.

Part Three will introduce the strategies and methods that enable organizations to secure their CPM environments through ITPCS Unification without disrupting business operations. Here this Series takes the challenge Insider Threat Prevention Cyber Terror head-on by introducing the vision of a Unified Continuous Performance Management and Insider Threat Prevention Cyber Security architecture derived from Behavioral Science.

Collectively, The Psychology of Insider Threat Prevention Cyber Security Series examines the behavioral, social, technical, philosophical, managerial, strategic and operational considerations of such a large-scale program. It addresses the challenge of building new workplace relationships in organizations designed to combat Cyber Terror by building Insider Threat Prevention Cyber Security effectiveness in any organization.

Future Volumes will examine the core components of any Insider Threat Prevention Cyber Security Program including Leadership, Communication, Training & Development, Governance, Risk Management, and Control.

Description of Terms

Cardinal Virtues: Virtues are positive behaviors that become habits. The Cardinal Virtues include Justice, Fidelity, Self-Care, and Prudence. They are referred to as "Cardinal" because they are the hinges that lead to all the virtues.

Computer Performance Evaluation (CPE): CPE is rigorous engineering experiment design to test the performance, reliability and capacity of an integrated computer system according to redefined external and internal acceptance criteria.

Design Inquiry: Iterative exploration of the systems, environments, spaces, dynamics, and models of design as the appropriate design inquiry architecture to produce a solution as a future system.

Dillon (1983) sees methodologies as imperfect. He argues that "Each is a product of the human mind and each is intended to bring some order out of the bewildering array of signals coming from the expanded sensory system. Each can form a mental image or model of the thing or event perceived, again it must be emphasized, from a particular perspective" (p. 11).

Existential Hunger: The innate and natural desire for union with other human beings. This refers to the human desire and capacity to form mutual relationships with human beings in a one-to-one and one-to-many correspondence, such as Social Connectivity, peer acceptance, affirmation.

Functional Relationship: Relationships in which human beings work together to achieve a mutual purpose or goal, as when sharing a social or professional project.

Human Activity System: A system in which the components are human beings engaging in processes of input, output, transformation, and feedback and adjustment.

Human Activity System Continua: The continuum of Human Activity Systems from open to closed, complex to simple (restricted), unitary to pluralist, and mechanistic to systemic.

Human Relationship Process Model: A relationships model that employs a Human Activity Systems view of transformation and growth.

Manipulative Relationship: A relationship emerging from Type One Existential Hunger in which other people are seen as means to an end regardless of the personal cost involved.

Metamethodology: METAM is a methodology for designing methodologies; HAS engage a MetaM to design a methodology appropriate to the type of HAS that is to be designed as an Information Systems. The MetaM is beyond any methodology. Close ties exist between methodologies and MetaM. Both Banathy and Checkland offer examples of MetaM. While Banathy (1989a) discussed a strategy for Design Inquiry as the design of design, Checkland (1981) offers a system for generating methodologies.

Methodologies are valuable in that any advance in science is preceded by advances in methodology (Misiak & Sexton, 1966; Branden, 1974). However, "advances in methodology are preceded by advances in philosophy" (Newkirk, 1991, p. 34). For me, a MetaM is "a generalization of all methodologies as a second level abstraction to provide a MetaM of all methodologies" (Newkirk, 1991a, p. 28).

MetaM rest on the bedrock of philosophical exploration and development. MetaM are required to design methodologies appropriate to a given problem situation. They are based on theory and practice, enhance system's evolution, organize methodologies, facilitate embedded systems building and support multiple paradigms (Newkirk, 1991a).

Methodology: A methodology can be hard or soft. Banathy (1988a) writes that a methodology "is defined as a set of coherent, related, and internally consistent methods applicable to pursuing disciplined inquiry" (p. 27). Checkland (1981) viewing methodology praxiologically, argues that "a methodology will lack the precision of a technique but will be a firmer guide to action than a philosophy" (p. 162). Flood and Carson (1988) discuss hard and soft systems methodologies by arguing that hard methodologies "set out to select an efficient means of achieving a known and defined end" (p. 107).

Ontologically, as a second level abstraction, the meta-methodology exists in the province of mathematics; retains intelligible matter; separates from common sensible matter; has the imagination as its end point; is a contingent system in that it cannot exist without individual sensible matter; and cannot be understood without intelligible matter (Hickey, 1976).

Focusing on systems, Collen (1985) argues: "A systemic method is a formalized means of studying a system" (p. 536). He continues by arguing that "system methodology is the study of such methods, as well as the collective applications of such methods to the study of a human activity system" (p. 536).

Methodology building is a design situation. It requires a design system to function as a methodology generating system, a HAS that engages a METAM to conduct Design Inquiry. To design a methodology, the designer must employ a METAM

Newkirk Model of Workplace Relationships: The Relationship Model of Dr. Raymond L. Newkirk that establishes Existential Hunger as the driving force energizing the formation of all human relationships from Type One to Type Four.

Objective Relationship: A relationship derived from Type One Existential Hunger that depersonalized members in the relationship by using them as objectives for attainment of goals.

Paradigm: Provides our perception of the world, how it works and what it contains in any given situation. We perceive the world within one world view or another which establishes any paradigm we may advocate for problem solving. Carrico (1989) describes a paradigm as a representation for the internal model that human beings employ to think about something. For Kuhn (1970), paradigms "define the legitimate problems and methods of a research field" (p. 10). Powers (1984), similar to Carrico above, argues that a paradigm "is a basic image which acts as an organizing and filtering agent, a socially accepted way of seeing, modelling, and communicating about reality" (p. 2).

Powers sees a paradigm as a larger system consisting of three crucial subsystems: ontological, methodological, and epistemological. As a systemist, I see a paradigm as a suprasystem consisting of ontological, epistemological, and psychological subsystems which together inform a metamethodology for making sense out of the world. Our paradigms influence our efforts at designing our own futures through design inquiry.

Carrico (1989) reasons that a paradigm serves as the representation for the internal model that we employ to think about something. Kuhn (1970) reasons that paradigms "define the legitimate problems and methods of a research field" (p. 10). Powers (1984) see a paradigm as a large philosophical system. As a systemist, I see a paradigm as a suprasystem consisting of ontological, epistemological and psychological subsystems which together inform a metamethodology as a design inquiry for making sense out of the world. Our paradigm influences our efforts of designing on own future through design inquiry. Others see paradigms as metaphorical (Morgan, 1986).

Principles, Laws, Corollaries and Guidelines: The Systems Approach is operationalized through its various dictates, assumptions, pre-suppositions, and guiding notions as expressed in the form of principles, laws, corollaries and guidelines (Yourdon, 1989a). This "legal" and "disciplined" foundation derived from GST stresses the nature of the systems approach as an expanded encounter with the world being perceived in the form of dynamical systems in interaction and interdependence through the interconnectedness of subsystems rather than as a background of static, discrete and non-interrelated components in isolation (Yourdon, 1989a).

An important corollary of the system approach is that as systems thinkers, we come to appreciate the uniqueness of an entity as a member of any system. If it is correct that a system is changed whenever a component or subsystem enters the system or leaves it, the component must be unique (Mayon-White and Morris, 1982). From the human science perspective studying both the expanded domain of HAS and the discrete organization structures and functions of traditional Organization Development, this corollary defends the uniqueness and indispensability of every person. Every human person brings something unique into their systems. This something unique makes the system other than what it previously was (Mayon-White & Morris, 1982).

The axioms, propositions, principles, laws, corollaries, and guidelines of the system approach are derived from the basic definition of the concept system. Bertalanffy (1950), Ashby (1956), Miller (1956), Checkland (1981), Myon-White and Morris (1983), Bogdanov (1984), Christakis (1985) and Warfield (1987) have all made their contributions. As the system movement evolves, the laws and principles developed within this perspective will gain increasing weight and influence. Although the dictates of the systems perspective lack empirical credibility, experience with them indicates that they contain logical content.

Checkland (1981) reasons that: "As the use of systems concepts in problem-solving is developed we may expect a parallel emergence of laws deriving from the logic of the use of systems ideas" (p. 234). These systems ideas are derived from the various systems perspectives that are evolving as a new paradigm of disciplined inquiry. Systems principles are implicit in many new theories of corporate rebirth.

Level One Existential Hunger: Fundamental human drive that leads to the formation of self-centered relationships.

Level Two Existential Hunger: Higher-level human drive to form relationships in which people may participate in attaining mutual goals.

Level Three Existential Hunger: Higher-Level human drive to form relationships in which the categories of love emerge as human beings become ends in themselves rather than means to ends.

Level Four Existential Hunger: Highest level of human relationship in which human beings seek out and pursue transformation of values and activities to experience deepest meanings of life, love, and relationships.

System: Mayon-White and Morris (1982) argue that a system is an assembly of components of particular interest to someone that are connected in an organized way for doing something. The components are affected by being in the system in such a way that the system is changed if any component leaves it. Systems are classified as natural system, designed systems, human activity systems, and social systems. Systems can be either hard or soft, designed physical systems or designed abstract systems. Some even authorities claim that systems exist which are beyond human knowledge; these are the transcendental systems (Checkland, 1981). In LST (Miller, 1988), systems consist of 19 subsystems.

Systems Design and Relevant Dynamics: Systems Design is a disciplined inquiry consisting of specialized techniques, general rules and universal principles. Banathy (1984) writes that "design is creative, disciplined, and decision-oriented inquiry carried out in iterative cycles. During these cycles, we develop design solutions by exploring three `spaces' that surround the design solution space: (a) the design knowledge space, (b) the design problem space, and (c) the design exploration space" (pp. 1-11).

Design systems work within the spaces of design to produce a desired system. Collen (1990) reasons that "Systems design is an ongoing activity which requires the participation of all stakeholders if a HAS is to evolve" (p.

4). Collen refers to the systems design methodology as the "Systems Design Journey" (p. 4) to reflect the continuous or evolutionary nature of design as distinct from planning.

The evolutionary nature of design flows from the dynamics occurring within the design experience. Two significant dynamics of design have been identified by Banathy (1984) as divergence and convergence. Design commences with an image of the future system and works to achieve it through iterations of divergence and convergence. The outcome of the design experience is a description of a new system to be implemented.

Spiritual Personal Relationship: A high-order relationship derived from Type Four Existential Hunger that leads individuals to personal-spiritual transformation and the attainment of uniquely spiritual values.

Systems Perspectives: The systems approach is engaged in a continuous debate. Debate rages over the very efficacy of the movement itself. Some fear that it may be just a new way of expressing old ideas. Others wonder if the systems approach is so general as to be vague, vacuous, and meaningless. Some argue over the best approach to systems. Just as the systems perspective is a way of perceiving the world, there exist several ways of perceiving systems.

Churchman (1979) writes that "the systems approach really consists of a continuing debate between various attitudes of mind with respect to society" (p. xi). He reasons that many systems debaters exist who fall into one of four classes of systems thinkers: (1) efficiency thinkers who study trouble spots; (2) science advocates who build objective models; (3) humanists who consider values while encouraging noninterference; (4) anti-planners who encourage experience at the expense of other rational approaches.

Workplace Relationships: Refers to associations and relationships formed in the workplace to meet personal and professional goals derived from Type One to Type Four Existential Hunger.

References & Historical Bibliography

This section provides a historical Reference and Bibliography that takes you back to the beginning when visions like Networked Information Systems, Continuous Performance Management and Insider Threat Prevention Cyber Security first began to emerge and brings you up to today. It introduces many of the thinkers and their ideas and concepts that informed the emergence and subsequent evolution of Insider Threat Prevention Cyber Security (ITPCS). At its best, ITPCS is a difficult discipline that, fortunately for us, has amassed a wonderful volume of insight over the years.

Mastery of the Psychology of Insider Threat Prevention Cyber Security is not an overnight project. Although each company suffers its own ITPCS concerns, they all share common challenges that elicit shared strategies and responses. As we have seen in Part One, Continuous Performance Management shares several Hallmarks that make ITP Cyber Security more difficult to enforce such as trust and openness and minimal management. Other organization initiatives and architectures have issues that also complicate the enforcement of ITP Cyber Security.

Many, if not most, people today are unaware of the breadth and depth of the conceptual universe that forms a viable, potent, and successful Insider Threat Prevention Cyber Security Program. Actually, several dozen disciplines come together to form resilient ITP Cyber Security. These range from Software Development, Program and Project Management, Hardware Systems Engineering, Budgeting, Finance, Strategic Thinking, Operations Management, Network Management, Version Control, and Human Resource Management to Behavioral Science, Sociology, Theology, Forensic Psychology, Personality and Trait theories, Systems Thinking, Human Activity Systems Design, Philosophy, Physics, Mathematics, Management, Organization Design, Enterprise Architecture Planning, Critical Theory, Ideology Critique, Training and Development, Communications, Methodology Design, Product Development and several others. I am sure you get the idea.

ITP Cyber Security is a complex challenge that people generally under-conceptualize. Getting it right demands significant change throughout the enterprise. The key word here is "PREVENTION". I am not talking about repair, correction, or making something less painful which is common with mitigation strategies. Mitigation is the effort to reduce loss of life and property by lessening the impact of disasters. II am speaking of Insider Threat Prevention Cyber Security. I mean stopping it in its tracks before it happens. This is hard to do, but it can be done.

Insider Threat Prevention is essential because such malicious insider attacks can destroy an entire enterprise in a very, very short time. While external intrusions are dangerous, very expense, and threatening, they rarely destroy an entire enterprise. Organizations recover from them. ITP Cyber Security is far difference because an increasing percentage of them render their targets useless, forever. Executive shave to think differently about Insider Threats, and implement enterprise architecture that actually prevent them while concurrently enhancing business operations. Success in the ear of Cyber Terror is indeed the brave new world.

As you understand more clearly the danger of insider attacks, you will also begin to recognize how complex this problem really is. Many disciplines come together to produce an Architecture that unifies enterprise models and Insider Threat Prevention Cyber Security models. An effective ITP Cyber Security solution presents a challenge of environmental unification that is well beyond the common practices of systems integration. This requires a knowledge base derived from the contribution of the thirty plus disciplines identified above.

-A –

Aamodt, Agnar: A Knowledge-Intensive, Integrated Approach to Problem Solving and Sustained Learning.

Ackoff, R. L. (1979, July). The Future of Operational Research is Past. In R. E. Cavallo (Ed.),

Systems Research Movement: Characteristics, Accomplishments and Current Developments. Binghampton, NY: Society for General Systems Research.

Ackoff, R.L. (1981). Creating the Corporate Future. New York: John Wiley & Sons.

Ackoff, R. L. (1982). On the Hard Headedness and Soft Headedness of M. C. Jackson. Journal of Applied Systems Analysis, 9.

Ackoff, R. L. (1991). Ackoff's Fables: Irreverent Reflections on Business and Bureaucracy. New York: John Wiley & Sons, Inc.

Ackoff, R. L., & Emery, Fred E. (1972). On Purposeful Systems. Seaside, CA: Intersystems Publications.

Adam, Nabil R. & Wortmann, John C. (1989, December). Security-Control Methods for Statistical Analysis

Adams, Kevin: Towards a System of Systems Methodologies, Once Again. Old Dominion University.

Adams, Kevin (2012): Systems Theory: A Formal Construct for Understanding Systems. Old Dominion University.

Amabile, Teresa M. (1983). The Social Psychology of Creativity. New York: Springer-Verlay

Andrews, Gregory R. (1991, March). Paradigms for Process Interaction in Distributed Programs. ACM Computing Surveys, 23 (1), pp. 49-90.

Andriole, Stephen J. (1985). Applications in Artificial Intelligence. Princeton: Petrocelli Books.

Andriole, Stephen J. (1986a). Microcomputer Decision Support Systems: Design, Implementation and Evaluation. Wellesley, MA: QED Information Sciences.

Andriole, Stephen J. (Ed.) (1986b). Software Validation, Verification, Testing and Documentation. Princeton: Petrocelli Books.

Annual Threat Report (2018). Produced by eSentire Threat Intelligence.

Anton, Corey (2015). A Heuristic Sketch of Lee Thayer's Systems Theory Orientation to Human Communication: Reflections on the Range of Open Systems. Grand Valley State University,

Aquinas, Thomas, Saint (1952). The Summa Theologica. Daniel J. Sullivan (Tr.). Chicago: The University of Chicago (The Great Books Edition), William Benton Publisher, Encyclop. Britt.

Aquinas, Saint Thomas, De Veritate, Summa Theologiae, I, q. 14.

Aquinas, Thomas, St.: Summa Theologica, I, Q. 85. Art 7.

Argyris, C; Schön, Donald A. (1985) Strategy, Change and Defensive Routines. Ballinger: Cambridge, MA.

Argyris, Cris (1970). Intervention Theory and Method. Reading, MA: Addison-Wesley.

Argyris, Chris, et al., (1985). Action Science. San Francisco: Jossey-Bass.

Aristotle (1952). Works of Aristotle. W. D. Ross (Ed.), 12 Vols. Oxford: Clarendon, Press.

Armstrong, A. H. (1949). An Introduction to Ancient Philosophy. Chicago: Newman Press.

Arraj, James. Jungian Spirituality: The Question of Victor White, Spirituality Today, Autumn 1988, Vol. 40 No. 3, pp. 249-261.

Ashby, W.R. (1956). An Introduction to Cybernetics. London: Chapman and Hall.

Ashby, W.R. (1958). Requisite Variety and Its Implications for the Control of Complex Systems. Cybernetics, 1, pp. 1-17

Association For Computing Machinery. (1990, October). Proceedings of the Conference on Computer-Supported Cooperative Work, October 7-10, 1990 Los Angeles, CA. Sponsored by ACM SIGCHI & SIGOIS.

Augustine, of Hippo (1981). Basic Writings of St. Augustine. Oates & Whitney (Tr.). New York: Baker Books.

Auletta, Gennaro (2005). The Trialistic Structure in Physics, Spiritual Information: 100 Perspectives on Science and Religion, Charles L. Harper, Jr. ed. Philadelphia, PA: Templeton Foundation Press, 2005.

Austin, Charles F. (1966). Management's Self-Inflicted Wounds: A Formula for Managerial and Executive Self-Analysis. New York: Holt, Rinehart and Winston.

Ayer, Steve J. & Patrinostro, Frank S. (1992). Software Configuration Management Identification, Accounting, Control, & Management. New York: McGraw-Hill, Inc.

-B-

Baker, Richard H. (1985). The Computer Security Handbook. Blue Ridge Summit, PA: TAB Professional and Reference Books.

Banathy, Bela (1973). Developing a Systems View of Education. Seaside, CA: Intersystems Publications.

Banathy, Bela (1979). The Dynamics of Integrative Design. General Systems Research, a Science, a Methodology, a Technology. Louisville: Society for General Systems Research.

Banathy, Bela (1983). Systems Behavior. San Francisco: Saybrook Institute.

Banathy, Bela (1984). Systems Design in the Context of Human Activity Systems. San Francisco: International Systems Institute.

Banathy, Bela (1986a). The Design of Design Inquiry in the Context of Human Activity Systems. San Francisco: Far West laboratory for Educational Research and Development.

Banathy, Bela (1986b, October). A Systems View of Development. U.N. Educational, Scientific and Cultural Organization Symposium: Meeting of experts on goals of development. Budapest.

Banathy, Bela (1987a). The Design of Evolutionary Guidance Systems. San Francisco: Saybrook

Banathy, Bela (1987b). The Characteristics and Acquisition of Evolutionary Competence. World Futures, 23, pp. 123-144.

Banathy, Bela (1987c). Choosing Design Methods. San Francisco: Far West Laboratory & Saybrook Graduate School.

Banathy, Bela (1988a). Matching Design Methods to System Type. San Francisco: Saybrook Institute.

Banathy, Bela (1988b). Goals of Development. Paris: U.N. Educational, Scientific and Cultural Organization.

Banathy, Bela (1989a). Design: A Journey to Create the Future, A Map Of The Journey. Carmel: Far West Laboratory and Saybrook Institute.

Banathy, Bela (1989b). The Design of Evolutionary Guidance Systems. Systems Research, 4.

Banathy, Bela (1990). Design: A Journey to Create the Future, A Map of The Journey. R. Trappi (Ed.), Cybernetics and Systems, 1990: Proceedings of the Tenth European Meeting on Cybernetics and Systems Research. Singapore: World Scientific, pp. 197-204.

Banathy, Bela (1991). Systems Design of Education: A Journey to Create the Future. Englewood Cliffs: Educational Technology Publications.

Banathy, B. H. & Mills, S. R. (1985). The Application of Living Systems Process Analysis in Education. ISI Monograph 85(7), pp. 1-16.

Barr, Avron & Feigenbaum, Edward A. (1981). The Handbook of Artificial Intelligence, Volume 1. Los Altos, CA: William Kaufmann, Inc.

Barr, Avron & Feigenbaum, Edward A. (1982). The Handbook of Artificial Intelligence, Volume 2. Los Altos, CA: William Kaufmann, Inc.

Bateson, Gregory (1973). Steps to an Ecology of Mind. London: Paladin.

Bateson, Gregory (1979). Mind and Nature: A Necessary Unity. New York: E. P. Sutton.

Beckhard, Richard (1967). The Confrontation Meeting. Harvard Business Review, XLV (2), 149-153.

Beckhard, Richard (1969). Organization Development: Strategies and Models. Reading, MA: Addison-Wesley Publishing Company.

Beckhard, Richard & Harris, Reuben (1977). Organizational Transitions: Managing Complex Change. Reading, MA: Addison-Wesley Publishing Company.

Beckhard, Richard & Pritchard, Wendy (1992). Changing the Essence: The Art of Creating and Leading Fundamental Change in Organizations. San Francisco: Jossey Bass Publishers.

Bellefontaine, Elizabeth. A Spirituality of Meaningful Experiences: Some Biblical Lesson, Spirituality Today, Autumn 1988, Vol. 40 No. 3, PP. 196-207.

Bennett, Roger (1989). Personal Effectiveness. London: Kogan Page Ltd.

Bennis, Warren (1969). Organization Development: Its Nature, Origins, and Prospects. Reading, MA: Addison-Wesley Publishing Company.

Bennis, Warren (1989a). Why Leaders Can't Lead: The Unconscious Conspiracy Continues. San Francisco: Jossey-Bass Publishers.

Bennis, Warren (1989b). On Becoming a Leader. Menlo Park: Addison-Wesley Publishing Company.

Bennis, Warren & Nanus, Burt (1985). Leaders: The Strategies for Taking Charge. New York: Harper & Row, Publishers.

Bernstein, R. J. (1983) Beyond Objectivism and Relativism. Basil Blackwell: Oxford.

Bertalanffy, L. von (1950). The Theory of Open Systems in Physics and Biology. Emery (Ed.) (1969) Systems Thinking. Harmondsworth, England: Penguin.

Bertalanffy, L. von (1968). General Systems Theory. New York: Braziller.

Beruvides, Mario Ph.D. & Cantu, Jaime (2013). Isomorphological Analysis: The Theory of It All. Texas Tech University

Boehm, B. A. (1981). Software Engineering Economics. Englewood Cliffs: Prentice-Hall, Inc.

Bogdanov, A. (1984). Essays in Tektology:The General Science of Organization. Seaside, CA: Intersystems Publications.

Boghossian, Paul A. (2007). Fear of Knowledge: Against Relativism and Constructivism. Oxford, England: Oxford University Press.

Boulding, Kenneth E. (1985). Human Betterment. Beverley Hills: Sage Publications.

Bowers, Todd, David. An Ontology for a Critical Systems Paradigm. Thesis submitted for the

M.Phil./Ph.D. Upgrade. Centre for Systems Studies, Hull U. Business School. California State Polytechnic U. at Pomona January, 2009

Bowers, Todd D. (2008) An Ontology for a Critical Systems Paradigm. Ph.D. Upgrade. Hull University Business School, Unpublished.

Bowers, Todd D. (2011) Ontological Support for Multiparadigm Multimethodologies: Isomorphic Process–Structures and the Critical Moment. Proceedings of the 54th Meeting of the International Society for the Systems Sciences. The International Society for the Systems Sciences: Hull, U.K.

Bowers, Todd D. Ph.D. (2012) Towards a Framework for Multiparadigm Multimethodologies. Centre for Systems Studies, Hull University Business School, University of Hull: Hull.

Bowers, Todd David, Ph.D: Developments in Critical Systems Theory: On Paradigms and Incommensurability Universidad del Norte – Barranquilla

Bowker, John W. (2005). God, Spiritual Information, and Downward Causation, Spiritual Information 100 Perspectives on Science and Religion, Charles L. Harper, Jr. (Ed.). Philadelphia, PA: Templeton Foundation Press. (pp. 479-483).

Boyd, Robert, D. & Myers, J. Gordon. Overcoming Leadership Scarcity: Discerning the Spiritual Journey, Spirituality Today, Autumn 1987, Vol. 39, pp. 225-240.

Branden, Nathaniel (1973). The Psychology of Self-Esteem. New York: Bantam Books.

British Telecommunications plc: How We Stay Ahead of a Changing Threat Landscape. (2018) Registered office: 81 Newgate Street, London EC1A 7AJ.

Bucker, Bill (2003). Spiritual Development and the Epistemology of Systems Theory, Journal of Psychology and Theology Vol. 31, 2003

Burrell, Gibson &Morgan, Gareth (1979) Sociological Paradigms and Organizational Analysis. Heinemann: London. Management Science, 17, B37–B53.

-C-

Capra, Fritjof (1982). The Turning Point. New York: Simon & Schuster

Capra, Fritjof (1991). The Tao of Physics, third edition. Boston: Shambhala.

Capra, Fritjof and Steindl-Rast (with Thomas Matus) (1991). Belonging to the Universe. San Francisco: Harper.

CERT National Insider Threat Center. Common Sense Guide to Mitigating Insider Threats, Sixth Edition. December 2018

Checkland, Peter B. (1981). Systems Thinking, Systems Practice. Wiley: Chichester.

Christakis, A. N. (1981). High Technology Participative Design: The Space Based Laser. Proceedings of the Annual Meeting, Society for General Systems Research. Louisville, KY.

Churchman, C. West (1970). Operations Research as a Profession.

Churchman, C. W. (1971). The Design of Inquiring Systems. New York: John Wiley & Sons.

Churchman, C. W. (1979a). The Systems Approach and Its Enemies. New York: Basic Books. Churchman, C. W. (1979b). The Systems Approach. New York: Dell Publishing Company.

Churchman, C. W. (Ed.) (1989). The Well-Being of Organizations. Seaside, CA: Intersystems Publications.

Codd, E. F. (1990). The Relational Model for Database Management, Version 2. Menlo Park: Addison-Wesley Publishing Company.

Collen, Arne (1985). Experimental Method within Systems Methodology: The Case For and Against. B. Banathy, (Ed.). Proceedings of the Society for General Systems Research, 1, pp. 536-539.

Collen, Arne (1987, October). Living Systems Process Analysis for Program Evaluation. A paper presented at the annual meeting of the American Evaluation Association in Boston.

Collen, Arne (1988, May). Living Systems Methodology for Organizational Design and Redesign. Paper presented at the meetings of the International Society for General Systems Research, St. Louis, Missouri.

Collen, Arne (1990, April 10). Evolutionary Guidance Systems and Systems Design. A paper presented at the Tenth European Meeting on Cybernetics and Systems Research in Vienna.

Collen, Arne (1992). Methodological Perspectives on Human Systems, Design, and Learning for a More Global Ethic. San Francisco: Saybrook Institute.

Collen, Arne, Ph.D. & Newkirk, Raymond L. (1992). Cybernetics, Living Systems Theory, and Organizational Behavior. San Francisco & Concord, California: Saybrook Institute & Systems Management Institute (Paper for 13th international Congress on Cybernetics).

Collins, Robin A. (2005). Design and the Designer, Spiritual Information: 100 Perspectves on Science and Religion, Charles L. Harper, Jr. ed. Philadelphia, PA: Templeton Foundation Press.

Conrad, James W. (1988). Handbook of Communications Systems Management. Boston: Auerbach Publishers, Inc.

Conrad, James W. (1989). Handbook of Communications Systems Management, 1989 Yearbook. Boston: Auerbach Publishers, Inc.

Conrad, James W. (1990a). Handbook of Communications Systems Management, 1990-1991 Yearbook. Boston: Auerbach Publishers, Inc.

Conrad, James W. (1990b). Handbook of Communications Systems Management: Communications Standards. Boston: Auerbach Publishers, Inc.

Craig & Houston-Ludlam (1989, May 25). A Psychological Framework for Testing. Sixth International Conference on Testing Computer Software, Ann Harbor, MI: Tec-Ed Technical Publications and Graphics Services.

Csanyi, Vilmos (1982). General Theory of Evolution. Budapest: Akademiai Kiado.

-D-

Databases: A Comparative Study. ACM Computing Surveys, 21(4), pp. 515-556.

Davidow, William H. & Malone, Michael S. (1992). The Virtual Corporation: Structuring and Revitalizing the Corporation for the 21st Century. New York: Harper Collins Publishers.

Davino, Louis. Francis of Assisi: Metaphor of Franciscan Maturity, Spirituality Today, Autumn 1987, Vol. 39, pp. 241-249.

Defense Systems Management College (1986a). Risk Management Concepts and Guidance. Fort Belvoir, VA: Defense Systems Management College.

Defense Systems Management College (1986b). Integrated Logistics Support Guide. Fort Belvoir, VA: Defense Systems Management College.

Defense Systems Management College (1987). Guide for the Management of Multinational Programs. Fort Belvoir, VA: Defense Systems Management College.

Defense Systems Management College (1988). Test and Evaluation Management Guide. Fort Belvoir, VA: Defense Systems Management College.

Defense Systems Management College (1989a). Defense Manufacturing Management: Guide for Program Managers Fort Belvoir, VA: Defense Systems Management College.

Defense Systems Management College (1989b). Systems Engineering Management Guide. Fort Belvoir, VA: Defense Systems Management College.

Defense Systems Management College (1990). Scheduling Guide for Program Managers. Fort Belvoir, VA: Defense Systems Management College.

Denton, Michael, J. (2005). Henderson's Fine-Tuning Argument, Spiritual Information: 100 Perspectives on Science and Religion, Charles L. Harper, Jr. ed. Philadelphia, PA: Templeton Foundation Press, 2005.

Derek Melber, MVP (2020): Detecting Insider Threats and Attacks, Manage Engine Special Edition. John Wiley & Sons, New Jersey, 2020

Dickinson, Brian (1980). Developing Structured Systems: A Methodology Using Structured Techniques. New York: Yourdon Press.

Dickinson, Brian (1989). Developing Quality Systems: A Methodology Using Structured Techniques. New York: McGraw-Hill Book Company.

Dinsmore, Paul C. (1984). Human Factors in Project Management. New York: American Management Association Publications Group.

Domb, Ellen & Rantanen, Kalevi (2002): 40 Principles for Innovative Problem Solving. TRIZ, CRC Press.

Doohan, Leonard. Current Trends Scripture and Contemporary Spirituality, Spirituality Today, Spring 1990, Vol. 42 No. 1, pp. 62-74.

Downey, Michael. Current Trends Understanding Christian Spirituality: Dress Rehearsal for a Method, Spirituality Today, Fall 1991, Vol. 43 No. 3, pp. 271-280.

Drack, Manfred & Pouvreau, David (2006). On the History of Ludwig von Bertalanffy's "General Systemology", and on Its Relationship to Cybernetics Part I: Elements on the Origins and Genesis of Ludwig von Bertalanffy's "General Systemology." International Journal of General Systems, 44:5, 523-571,

Drack, Manfred & Pouvreau, David (2015). On the History of Ludwig Von Bertalanffy's "General Systemology", and on Its Relationship to Cybernetics – Part III: Convergences and Divergences. International Journal of General Systems, 44:5, 523-571, DOI:

Drucker, Peter (1989). The New Realities. New York: Harper & Row Publishers.

Drucker, Peter (1992). Managing for the Future: The 1990s and Beyond. New York: Truman Talley Books/Dutton.

Duffey, Michael K. Called to be Holy: The Reconvergence of Christian Morality and Spirituality, Spirituality Today, Winter 1986, Vol. 38, pp. 349-360.

-E-

Ellis, George, F.R. Progress in Scientific and Spiritual Understanding, Spiritual Information 100 Perspectives on Science and Religion, Charles L. Harper, Jr. ed. Philadelphia, PA: Templeton Foundation Press, 2005, pp. 130-131.

Emery, F. E. (1967). The Next Thirty Tears: Concepts, Methods and Anticipations. Human Relations 20(3), pp.199-237.

Emery, F. E. & Trist, E. L. (1960). Socio-Technical Systems. Management Science Models and Techniques, vol. 2. Churchman and Verhulst (Eds.). Oxford: Pergamon.

Emery, F. E. & Trist, E. L. (1973). Towards a Social Ecology: Appreciations of the Future in the Present. New York: Plenum.

-F-

Fals-Borda, O. Rahman, M.A. (1991) Action and Knowledge: Breaking the Monopoly with Participatory Action Research. Apex Press: New York.

Fensel, Dieter & Siorpaes, Katharina (2010): Intelligent Systems.

Fereidunian, Alireza e al: A Complex Adaptive System of Systems Approach to Human–Automation Interaction in Smart Grid. Smart Grid Lab, Faculty of Electrical Engineering, K. N. Toosi University of Technology,

Feyerabend, Paul (1993). Against Method, Third Edition. New York: Verso.

Flood, Robert L. (1989a). Archaeology of Systems Inquiry. Systems Practice., 2, 117-124.

Flood, Robert L. (1989b). Six Scenarios for the Future of Systems "Problem Solving". Systems Practice., 2, 75-99.

Flood, Robert L. (1990) Liberating Systems Theory. Plenum New York.

Flood, Robert L. (1993) Beyond TQM. Wiley:New York.

Flood, Robert L.; Jackson, Michael C. (1991) Critical Systems Thinking: Directed Readings. Wiley: Chichester.

Flood, Robert L.; Romm, Norma R. A. (1995a). Diversity Management: Theory in Action. Systems Practice, 8(4), 469.

Flood, Robert L: Romm, Norma R. A. (1995b) Enhancing the Process of Methodology Choice in Total Systems Intervention (TSI) and Improving Chances of Tackling Coercion. Systems Practice, 8(4), 377.

Flood, Robert L., Romm, Norma R. A. (1996): Critical Systems Thinking: Current Research and Practice. Plenum: New York ; London.

Florian, M. (1974). On the Teaching of Model Building: Mathematical Techniques and Data Analysis. B.A. Bayraktar, H. Muller-Merbach, J. E.

Fricchione, Gregory L. (2005). Of Monocytes and the Spiritual Man, Spiritual Information: 100 Perspectives on Science and Religion, Charles L. Harper, Jr. ed. Philadelphia, PA: Templeton Foundation Press, 2005, pp. 400-405.

-G-

Gabriel, Henmar (1990). Tools and Techniques of Project Management. Tucson, AZ: Probity Corp.

Gadamer, Hans-Georg (1975). Truth and Method. London: Sheed and Ward.

Galbraith, Jay (1973). Designing Complex Organizations. Reading, MA: Addison-Wesley Publishing Company.

Gasparski, Wojciech (1984). Understanding Design:The Praxeological–Systemic Perspective. Seaside, CA: Intersystems Publications.

Georgiou, Ion (2007) Thinking Through Systems Thinking. Routledge: London.

Glasersfeld, Ernst von (1995) Radical Constructivism: A Way of Knowing and Learning. Falmer Press: London.

Gleiser, Marcelo (2005). Emergent Realities in the Cosmos, Spiritual Information: 100 Perspectives on Science and Religion, Charles L. Harper, Jr. ed. Philadelphia, PA: Templeton Foundation Press, 2005.

Goguen, Tad (1986). Designing Learning Systems for Anxiety Management in Clinical Training Systems. San Francisco: Saybrook Institute (Unpublished Essay).

Goodenough, Ursula (1998). The Sacred Depths of Nature, New York, New York: Oxford Universitry Press.

Goodman, Nelson (1978). Ways of Worldmaking. Indianapolis, IN: Hackett Publishing

Green, Sara & Wolkenhauer, Olaf (2017). Tracing Organizing Principles: Learning from the History of Systems Biology. Stellenbosch Institute for Advanced Study (STIAS) Wallenberg Research Centre Stellenbosch University Marais Road, Stellenbosch, South Africa.

Gregory, Wendy J. Ph.D. (1992) Critical Systems Thinking and Pluralism: A New Constellation. Systems Science Department, The City University: London.

Gregory, Wendy J. (1996) Dealing with Diversity. In Flood, Robert L. and Romm, Norma R. A., eds. Critical Systems Thinking: Current Research and Practice. Plenum Press: New York, 37–61.

-H-

Habermas, Jürgen (1981) The Theory of Communicative Action: Vol. One. Reason and the Rationalization of Society. Polity Press: Cambridge.

Hacking, Ian (1999). The Social Construction of What? Cambridge, Mass: Harvard University Press.

Haidar, Diana, et al. Any Threat: An Opportunistic Knowledge Discovery Approach to Insider Threat Detection. December 4, 2018.

Halkes, Catherina. Feminism and Spirituality, Spirituality Today, Autumn 1988, Vol. 40 No. 3, pp. 220-236.

Hardon, John A., S.J. Contemporary Spirituality, Father John A. Hardon Archives, Conference Transcription from a Retreat. 2988. Inter Mirifica. The Real Presence Association, Inc. 7030 West 63rd Street, Chicago: Ill.

Harper, Charles, Jr. (ED.) (2005). Spiritual Information. Templeton Foundation Press, Philadelphia.

Held, David (1980). Introduction to Critical Theory: Horkheimer to Habermas. Berkeley: University of California Press.

Hodge, Richard. A Systems Approach to Strategy and Execution in National Security Enterprises. (PhD THESIS).Defence and Systems Institute, University of South Australia. 31 January 2010

Holt, Bradley P. (2005). Thirsty for God A Brief History of Christian Spirituality. Minneapolis, MINN: Fortress Press.

Hutchings, Alice, Clayton, Richard & Anderson, Ross: Taking Down Websites to Prevent Crime (2016). Computer Laboratory, University of Cambridge, Cambridge CB3 0FD

Huyssteen, J. Wentzel Van (2006). Alone in the World? Human Uniqueness in Science and Theology. William B. Eerdmans Publishing Company: Grand Rapids, Michigan.

-I-

Idinopulos, Thomas A. (1971). The Erosion of Faith an Inquiry Into the Origins of the Contemporary Crisis in Religious Thought. Quadrangle Books Inc., Chicago, Ill.

Ingvar, David (1985). Memory of the Future:An Essay on the Temporal Organization of Conscious Awareness, Human Neurobiol, 1985; 4: 127-36.

Ivanov, Kristo (1989b). Computer Applications and Organizational Disease. The Well-Being of Organizations, C. West Churchman (Editor). pp. 283-312. Salinas, CA: Intersystems Publications.

Ivanov, Kristo (1989c). Information Systems Design through Creativity: A Tutorial Route Towards Aesthetics and Ethics. Umea, Sweden: University of Umea: Institute of Information Processing Department of Administrative Data Processing.

Ivanov, Kristo (1990). Hypersystems: A Base for Specification of Computer-Supported Self-Learning Social Systems. Umea, Sweden: University of Umea: Institute of Information Processing Administrative Data Processing.

Ivanov, Kristo (1991a). Computer-Supported Human Science or Humanistic Computing Science? Steps Toward the Evaluation of a Humanistic Computing Science. Umea, Sweden: University of Umea: Institute of Information Processing Administrative Data Processing.

Ivanov, Kristo (1991b). Computer-Human Interaction as Continuous System Reconstruction. Umea, Sweden: University of Umea, Institute of Information Processing Administrative Data Processing.

Ivanov, Kristo (1991c). Artificial Intelligence in the Context of Cultural Crisis. Umea, Sweden: University of Umea, Institute of Information Processing, Administrative Data Processing.

Ivanov, Kristo (1987). Rule of Law in Information Systems Research: The Role of Ethics in Knowledge-Building Procedures, Especially, in the Updating of Inference Networks. Umea, Sweden: Umea University: Institute of Information Processing Administrative Data Processing.

Ivanov, Kristo (1989a). Ideas for Humanistic and Social Science Research about Consequences of the Increasing Use of Information Technology. Umea, Sweden: University of Umea: Institute of Information Processing.

-J-

Jackson, M. C.; Keys, P. (1984) Towards a System of Systems Methodologies. Operational Research Society, 35, 473-486.

Jackson, Michael C. (1985) Social Systems Theory and Practice: The Need for a Critical Approach. International Journal of General Systems.10, 135–151.

Jackson, Michael C. (1987). New Directions in Management Science. In Jackson, M. C. & Keys, P., eds. New Directions in Management Science. Gower: Aldershot, 133–164.

Jackson, Michael C. (1997) Pluralism in Systems Thinking and Practice. In Mingers, John C. & Gill, Anthony, eds. Multimethodology: The Theory and Practice of Combining Management Science Methodologies. John Wiley & Sons: Chichester, 347–378.

Jackson, Michael C. (1999) Towards Coherent Pluralism in Management Science. Journal of the Operational Research Society, 50, 12-22.

Jackson, Michael C. (2000) Systems Approaches to Management. Kluwer Academic/Plenum: New York, London.

Jaeger, Lydia (2005). Cosmic Order and Divine Word, Spiritual Information: 100 Perspectives on Science and Religion, Charles L. Harper, Jr. ed. Philadelphia, PA: Templeton Foundation Press, 2005.

Jantsch, E. (1976). Evolution and Consciousness. Reading, MA: Addison-Wesley.

Jantsch, E. (1981). The Evolutionary Vision. Boulder, CO: Westview Press.

Jantsch, E. & Waddington, C. H. (1976). Evolution and Consciousness: Human Systems in Transition. Reading, MA: Wiley.

Johnson-Laird, Philip N. (1988). The Computer and the Mind. Cambridge, MA: Harvard University Press.

Jones, Peter H., PhD (2013: Social Systems. OCAD University, Toronto,Canada. Accepted chapter in: Social Systems and Design, Gary Metcalf (editor). Volume 1 of the Translational Systems Science Series, Springer

-K-

Kallas, Endel. Spirituality on this Side of the Atlantic According to Alexis de Tocqueville, Spirituality Today, Winter 1985, Vol. 37, pp. 292-303.

Kaminsky, Donna Marie F. Secular Franciscans: Bearers of Peace, Messengers of Joy, Spirituality Today, Summer 1985, Vol. 37, pp. 120-129.

Kennan, James, F., S.J. (2004). Moral Wisdom: Lessons and Texts from the Catholic Tradition, Claretian Publications, Quezon City, Philippines

Kilpatrick, William (2012). Christianity, Islam, and Atheism: The Struggle for the Soul of the West. Ignatius Press, San Francisco

Klir, G. (1985). Architecture of Systems Problem Solving. New York: Plenum Press.

Klubertanz, George P., S. J. (1953). The Philosophy of Human Nature. New York: Appleton-Century Crofts, Inc.

Klubertanz, George P., S. J. (1955). Introduction to the Philosophy of Being. Englewood Cliffs: Prentice-Hall, Inc.

Korzybski, Alfred, Science and Sanity: An introduction to Non-Aristotelian Systems and General Semantics, Institute of General Semantics, Lakeville, Conn, 1933.

Kotarbinski, T. (1966). Gnosiology: The Scientific Approach to the Theory of Knowledge. Oxford: Pergamon

Kremer, J. W. (1986). The Human Science Approach as Discourse. The Saybrook Review, 6(1). Spring, pp. 65-106.

Krippner, Stanley, et al. (1985). Toward the Application of General Systems Theory in Humanistic Psychology. Systems Research, 2(2), pp. 105-115. London: International Federation for Systems Research, Pergamon Press Ltd.

Kuhn, T. S. (1970). The Structure of Scientific Revolutions. Chicago: University of Chicago Press.

Kuong, Javier F. (1987). Computer Auditing, Security & Internal Control Manual. Englewood Cliffs: Prentice-Hall, Inc

-L-

Land, George & Jarman, Beth (1992). Breakpoint and Beyond: Mastering the Future - Today. New York: Harper Business.

Lane, Byron (1985). Managing People. Sunnyvale, CA: Oasis press.

Langsam, Jude. The Discalced Carmelite Secular Order: One Member's View, Spirituality Today, Summer 1985, Vol. 37, pp. 130-139.

Lantz, Kenneth E. (1986). The Prototyping Methodology. Englewood Cliffs: Prentice-Hall

Laszlo, Ervin (1972a). Introduction to Systems Philosophy. New York: Gordon & Breach; Harper Torchbooks (2nd ed. 1973).

Laszlo, Ervin (1972b). The Systems View of the World. New York: George Braziller.

Lawler, Edward E. III & Rhode, John Grant (1976). Information and Control in Organizations. Pacific Palisades, CA: Goodyear Publishing Company, Inc.

Lecarme, Olivier & Gart, Mireille Pellissier (1986). Software Portability. New York: McGraw-Hill Book Company.

Lehman, M. M. (1980, September). Programs, Life Cycles, and Laws of Software Evolution. Proceedings of the IEEE, 68(9), pp. 1060-1076.

LeShan, Lawrence, Ph.D. (1990). The Dilemma of Psychology: A Psychologist Looks at His Troubled Profession. New York: Penguin Books.

Levenson, Edgar A. (1972). The Fallacy of Understanding: An Inquiry into the Changing Structure of Psychoanalysis. New York: Basic Books, Inc.

Levin, Ben: (2013) The Simple Art of Governing Complex Systems. University of Toronto.

Levinson, Harry (1972). Organizational Diagnosis. Cambridge: Harvard University Press.

Lewis, David & Greene, James (1982). Thinking Better. New York: Rawson, Wade Publishers.

Lewton, Joel, C. Reformed Spirituality: Towards the Development of a Transcendent Community, Spirituality Today, Autumn 1989, Vol. 41 No. 3, pp. 213-225.

Lightedge (2016): Cyberattack Threat and Prevention: Protecting Your Organization Can Be Easy for You.

Linde, Andrei (2005). Choose Your Own Universe, Spiritual Information 100 Perspectives On Science and Religion, Charles L.

Litterer, Joseph A. (1973). The Analysis of Organizations. New York: John Wiley & Sons.

Lobel, Jerome (1986). Foiling the System Breakers: Computer Security and Access Control. New York: McGraw-Hill Book Company.

Lundell, Jay & Notess, Mark (1991). Human Factors in Software Development: Models, Techniques, and Outcomes. Human Factors in Computing Systems: Reaching through Technology, CHI '91 Conference Proceedings. Robertson, Scott P., Olson, Gary M., & Olson, Judith (Eds.). April-May, pp. 145-152. New Orleans, LA: ACM SIGCHI.

Lundy, James L. (1991). Lead, follow, or Get Out of the Way: Invaluable Insights into Leadership Style. Quezon City, Philippines: Kadena Press, University of the Philippines.

-M-

Maccoby, Michael (1988). Why Work: Motivating and Leading the New Generation. New York: Simon & Schuster.

Mackintosh, Hugh Ross (1937). Types of Modern Theology. New York, New York: Scribner's.

Macnaughton, Ian (1987). Design in the Context of Human Activity Systems. San Francisco: Saybrook Institute (Unpublished Essay).

Madala, S. & Sinclair, J. B. (1991, January). Performance of Synchronous Parallel Algorithms with Regular Structures. IEEE Transactions on Parallel and Distributed Systems, 2(1). Washington, D.C: IEEE Computer Society.

Magnin, Thierry (2005). Quantum Logic and the God-World Relationship: A New Resource for Exploring Modern Christian Theology, Spiritual Information: 100 Perspectives on Science and Religion, Charles L. Harper, Jr. ed. Philadelphia, PA: Templeton Foundation Press.

Mair, William C., Wood, Donald R., & Davis, Keagle W. (1972). Computer Control & Audit. Wellesley, MA: Q.E.D. Information Sciences, Inc.

Management Research Group (1983). Management Effectiveness Analysis. Portland, ME: Management Research Group.

Management Research Group (1987). Leadership Effectiveness Analysis: An Introductory Guide. Portland, ME: Management Research Group.

Manzini, Andrew O. (1988). Organizational Diagnosis: A Practical Approach to Company Problem Solving and Growth. New York: American Management Association.

Manzini, Andrew O. & Gridley, John D. (1986). Integrating Human Resources and Strategic Business Planning. New York: American Management Association.

Maritain, Jacque (1952). Range of Reason. New York: Charles Scribner & Sons.

Martel, Leon (1986). Mastering Change: The Key to Business Success. London: Grafton Books.

Martin, James (1973). Security, Accuracy and Privacy in Computer Systems.

Martin, James (1984). An Information Systems Manifesto. Englewood Cliffs: Prentice-Hall, Inc.

Martin, James (1985a). System Design from Provably Correct Constructs. Englewood Cliffs: Prentice-Hall, Inc.

Martin, James & McClure, Carma (1983). Software Maintenance: The Problem and Its Solutions. Englewood Cliffs: Prentice-Hall, Inc.

Martin, James & McClure, Carma (1988). Structured Techniques: The Basis of CASE. Englewood Cliffs: Prentice-Hall, Inc.

Martin, James & Oxman, Steven (1988). Building Expert Systems: A Tutorial. Englewood Cliffs: Prentice-Hall, Inc.

Marty, Martin E. If Theologians Do Not Measure, Can They Measure Up? Rules For Acquiring Spiritual Information, Spiritual Information 100 Perspectives On Science and Religion, Charles L. Harper, Jr. ed. Philadelphia, PA: Templeton Foundation Press, 2005, pp. 473-478.

Mattessich, Richard (1982). The Systems Approach: Its Variety of Aspects. Journal of the American Society for Information Science.

Maturana, Humberto R. (1988). Ontology of Observing: The Biological Foundations of Self-Consciousness.

Mayer, Michael (1984). The Mystery of Personal Identity. San Diego: ACS Publications, Inc.

McCabe, Thomas J. (1980). Software Quality Assurance: A Survey. Columbia, MD: McCabe & Associates.

McClelland, James L., Rumelhart, David E. & The PDP Research Group (1986). Parallel Distributed Processing: Explorations in the Microstructures of Cognition, Volume 2: Psychological and Biological Models. Cambridge, MA: The MIT Press.

McGinn, Bernard (2005). The Letter and the Spirit: Spirituality as an Academic Discipline, in Mind the Spirit: The Study of Christian Spirituality. Elizabeth A. Dreyer & mark S. Burrows (Eds.). Baltimore, MD: The Johns Hopkins University Press. pp. 25-41.

McKie, James W. (Ed.) (1974). Social Responsibility and the Business Predicament. Washington, D.C: The Brookings Institution.

McLean (1976). The Human Side of Systems: The User's Perspective. Presented at the Western Systems Conference. Los Angeles.

McMillan, Grant R., et al. (1989). Applications of Human Performance Models to System Design. New York: Plenum Press.

McNicholas, James B. III & Houssain Kettani (2019). Consideration of Insider Based Collusion Attacks on Cyber Systems.

Mercer, Michael W. (1989). Turning Your Human Resources Department Into a Profit Center. New York: AMACOM.

Merker, S. L. (1985). Living Systems Theory: A Framework for Management. Behavioral Science, 30, pp. 187-194.

Merker, S. L. (1986). Living Systems Process Analysis in the Far-East: A Review of Two Studies. Proceedings of the Society for General Systems Research, 1, G., pp. 42-51.

Metzger, Philip W. (1987). Managing Programming People: A Personal View. Englewood Cliffs: Prentice-Hall, Inc

McManus, Sonia, et al., (2017). Resilience Management: A Framework for Assessing and Improving the Resilience of Organizations. Resilient Organizations Research Report 2007/01 New Zealand

Midgley, Gerald (1989). Critical Systems: The Theory and Practice of Partitioning Methodologies. Proceedings of the 33rd Annual Meeting of the International Society for General Systems Research. Edinburgh.

Midgley, Gerald (1992). Pluralism and the Legitimation of Systems Science. Systems Practice, 5(2), 147-172.

Midgley, Gerald (1996). What Is This Thing Called CST? Flood, Robert. L. and Romm, N. R. A., eds. Critical Systems Thinking: Current Research and Practice. Plenum: New York, 11–24.

Midgley, Gerald (2000). Systemic Intervention: Philosophy, Methodology, and Practice. Kluwer Academic/Plenum: New York.

Midgley, Gerald (2011). Theoretical Pluralism in Systemic Action Research. Systems Practice and Action Research, 24(1), 1–15.

Miller, Eric (Ed.). (1991). Future Vision: The 189 Most Important Trends of the 1990s. Naperville, IL: Sourcebooks Trade.

Miller, G. A. (1978). The Magical Number Seven, Plus or Minus Two: Some Limits in Our Capacity for Processing Information. Psychology Review, 63(2), pp. 81-97.

Miller, J. G. (1978). Living Systems. New York: McGraw-Hill Book Company.

Miller, J. G. & Miller, J. L. (1980). The Family as a System. C. Hofling and J. Lewis (Eds.), The Family: Evaluation and Treatment, pp. 141-184, New York: Brunner/Mazel.

Miller, J. G. & Miller, J. L. (1989). A General Living Systems Analysis of Organizational Pathology. The Well-Being of Organizations, C. West Churchman (Ed.). Salinas, CA: Intersystems Publications.

Mills, D. Quinn (1991). Rebirth of the Corporation. New York: John Wiley & Sons, Inc.

Mingers, John C. (2000). The Contribution of Critical Realism as an Underpinning Philosophy for OR/MS and Systems. Journal of the Operational Research Society, 51(11), 12561270.

Mingers, John C. (2003). A Classification of the Philosophical Assumptions of Management Science Methods. Journal of the Operational Research Society, 54(6), 559-570 doi: 10.1057/palgrave.jors. 2601436|ISSN 0160-5682.

Mingers, John C. (2006). Realising Systems Thinking: Knowledge and Action in Management Science. Springer: New York.

Mishkoff, Henry C. (1985). Understanding Artificial Intelligence. Dallas: Texas Instruments.

Mitroff, I. I. & Kilmann, R. H. (1978). Methodological Approaches to Social Sciences. San Francisco: Jossey-Bass.

Mohrman, Susan Albers & Cummings, Thomas G. (1989). Self-Designing Organizations: Learning How to Create High Performance. Menlo Park, CA: Addison-Wesley Publishing Company.

Montalbano, Michael (1974). Decisions Tables. Chicago: Science Research Associates, Inc

Montazemi, Ali Reza & Gupta Kalyan Moy (2006): A Framework for Retrieval in Case-Based Reasoning Systems. School of Business, McMaster University, Hamilton, Ontario, Canada L8S 4M4

Montelibano, Joji & Andrew Moore (2012): Insider Threat Security Reference Architecture.

Morgan, Gareth (1986). Images of Organization. Sage: London.

Mowshowitz, A. (1976). The Conquest of Will: Information Processing in Human Affairs. Reading, MA: Addison-Wesley.

Muftic, Sead (1989). Security Mechanisms for Computer Networks. New York: Halstead Press, a Division of John Wiley & Sons.

Mulligan, Robert W., S. J. (1952). Truth: A Translation of Quaestiones Disputatae Deveritate, Questions I-IX of St.Thomas Aquinas. Chicago: Henry Regnery Company.

Murdoch, Iris (1992). Metaphysics as a Guide to Morals. New York, New York: The Penguin Press.

Murphy, Michael A. & Parker, Xenia Ley (1989). Handbook of EDP Auditing. Boston: Warren, Gorham & Lamont, Inc.

Murphy, Nancey, C. (2005). The Role of Discernment in Seeking Spiritual Knowledge, Spiritual Information: 100 Perspectves on Science and Religion, Charles L. Harper, Jr. ed. Philadelphia, PA: Templeton Foundation Press, 2005.

Musa, Iannino & Okumoto (1987). Software Reliability: Measurement, Prediction, and Application. New York: McGraw-Hill, Inc.

Myers, Glendord J. (1975). Reliable Software through Composite Design. New York: Van Nostrand Reinhold Company.

Myers, Glendord J. (1976). Software Reliability. New York: John Wiley & Sons.

-N-

Nadel, Robert B. (1987). Avoiding Micro-Computer Headaches: How to Control the Acquisition, Use, and Security Risks of Microcomputers. New York: McGraw-Hill Book Company.

Nadler, David A. (1977). Feedback and Organization Development: Using Data-Based Methods. Reading, MA: Addison-Wesley Publishing Company.

Nadler, Gerald (1967). Work Systems Design: The Ideals Concept. Homewood, IL: Richard D. Irwin, Inc.

Nadler, Gerald (1987). An Assessment of Systems Methodology and Design. B. H. Banathy (Ed.), Systems Inquiry, pp. 114-123. Louisville, KY: Society for General Systems Research.

Nadler, Gerald & Hibino, Shozo (1990). Breakthrough Thinking: Why We Must Change the Way We Solve Problems, and the Seven Principles to Achieve This. Rocklin, CA: Prima Publishing & Communications.

National Computer Security Center (1985). Personal Computer Security Considerations. Washington, D.C: National Computer Security Center.

National Computer Security Center (1988). Glossary of Computer Security Terms. Washington, D.C: National Computer Security Center.

Naughton, J. (1977). The Checkland Methodology: A Readers Guide, Second Edition. Milton Keynes: Open University Press.

Nemoto, Masao (1987). Total Quality Control for Management: Strategies and Techniques from Toyota and Toyoda Gosei. Englewood Cliffs: Prentice-Hall, Inc.

Newkirk, Raymond L. (2019). The Benefits of Human-Centered Insider Threat Prevention. Systems Management Institute Press. Orlando. FL.

Newkirk, Raymond L. (1976). The Descent of Man. New York: NYIT.

Newkirk, Raymond L. (1979). Preliminary Phased Development Process Plan. Fort Lauderdale, FL: Systems Engineering Laboratories.

Newkirk, Raymond L. (1981a). Preliminary Phased Documentation: An Overview. Fort Lauderdale, FL: Systems Engineering Laboratories.

Newkirk, Raymond L. (1981b). Phased Documentation Process: An Overview. Fort Lauderdale, FL: Systems Engineering Laboratories.

Newkirk, Raymond L. (1982). The Chronicles of the Making of a Philosopher: Book II, What is Philosophy? Fort Lauderdale, FL: Columbia Pacific University, (Master Thesis).

Newkirk, Raymond L. (1984a). Phased Development Process: An Overview. Jeddah, KSA: Royal Saudi Naval Forces.

Newkirk, Raymond L. (1984b). Project "A" Documentation Enhancement Plan. Jeddah, KSA: Royal Saudi Naval Forces (RSNF).

Newkirk, Raymond L. (1984c). The Process Philosophy of Project "A". Jeddah, KSA: RSNF.

Newkirk, Raymond L. & Reynolds, Michael L. (1984a). Phased Development Process: Project "A" Master Schedule. Jeddah, KSA: Royal Saudi Naval Forces.

Newkirk, Raymond L. & Reynolds, Michael L. (1984b). Phased Development Process: Project "A" Project Management Plan the Naval Supply Center Phased Automated Process. Jeddah, KSA: Royal Saudi Naval Forces.

Newkirk, Raymond L. & Reynolds, Michael L. (1984c). Phased Development Process: An Overview of the Project "A" Procedures Management Systems. Jeddah, KSA: RSNF.

Newkirk, Raymond L. & Reynolds, Michael L. (1984d). Phased Development Process: Project "A" Master Plan. Jeddah, KSA: Royal Saudi Naval Forces.

Newkirk, Raymond L. (1985a). Implementation Planning for Information Center Management, Vol.1. Quezon City, Philippine Islands: International Association for Information Management.

Newkirk, Raymond L. (1985b). Implementation Planning for Information Center Management, Vol. 2. Quezon City, Philippine Islands: International Association for Information Management.

Newkirk, Raymond L. (1985c). Phased Development Process Project "L" the Long-Range Plan for AFP: Automated Integrated Logistics Systems. Manila: IAIM.

Newkirk, Raymond L. (1986a). Post Implementation Review Handbook. Pleasant Hill, CA: (Pacific Bell MTS Project Document).

Newkirk, Raymond L. (1986b). Gestalt Training Process: Phased Training Plan Guidelines for Water and Sewer Customer Information and Billing System. San Francisco: IAIM.

Newkirk, Raymond L. (1987a). Post Implementation Review Handbook for Pacific Bell. San Ramon, CA: International Association of Information Management Press.

Newkirk, Raymond L. (1987b). A Systems Models Description of a Software Development System. San Francisco: Saybrook Institute.

Newkirk, Raymond L. (1988a). Operations Management in the 1990's. Pleasant Hill, CA: SMI.

Newkirk, Raymond L. (1988b). A Deductive Process Model of the Computer Software Development Human Activity System. Pleasant Hill, CA: Saybrook Institute.

Newkirk, Raymond L. (1988c). An LSPA Description of the Computer Software Development Human Activity System. San Francisco: Saybrook Institute.

Newkirk, Raymond L. (1988d). An Emerging Redesign of the Computer Software Development Human Activity System Using Living Systems Theory Guided by the Systems Models Approach. San Francisco: Saybrook Institute.

Newkirk, Raymond L. (1988e). Three Alternative Root Definitions of the Computer Software Development Human Activity System. San Francisco: Saybrook Institute

Newkirk, Raymond L. (1988f). A Conceptual Model of a Problem Situation Existing in the Software Development Human Activity System. San Francisco: Saybrook Institute

Newkirk, Raymond L. (1988g). A Project Proposal for the Design of a Computer Software Development Human Activity System. San Francisco: Saybrook Institute.

Newkirk, Raymond L. (1988h). The Nature and Characterization of Human Activity Systems in General and the Computer Software Development Human Activity System in Particular. San Francisco: Saybrook Institute.

Newkirk, Raymond L. (1988i). A Description of the Software Development Human Activity System. San Francisco: Saybrook Institute.

Newkirk, Raymond L. (1988j). A Comprehensive Characterization and Description of the Software Development Human Activity System. San Francisco: Saybrook Institute.

Newkirk, Raymond L. (1988k). Integrating Human Resource Planning with the Information Technology Business Plan: The Path to Contingency Planning. Pleasant Hill, CA: SMI.

Newkirk, Raymond L. (1989a). Capacity Management of the Corporate Computer System. Pleasant Hill, CA: Systems Management Institute Press.

Newkirk, Raymond L. (1989b). The Living Systems Approach: A New Software Design Paradigm for the 21st Century and Beyond. Pleasant Hill, CA: Saybrook Institute.

Newkirk, Raymond L. (1989c). Software Quality Assurance and Control. Pleasant-Hill, CA: Systems Management Institute.

Newkirk, Raymond L. (1989d). Design Operations and Tasks Leading to the Redesign of the Computer Software Development Human Activity System. San Francisco: Saybrook Institute.

Newkirk, Raymond L. (1989e). The Design System Supporting the Redesign of the Computer Software Development Human Activity System. San Francisco: Saybrook Institute.

Newkirk, Raymond L. (1989f). Developmental Objectives and Plans Supporting the Redesign of the Computer Software Development Human Activity System. San Francisco: Saybrook Inst.

Newkirk, Raymond L. (1989g). The Living Systems Approach a New Software Design Paradigm for the 21st Century and Beyond. San Francisco: Saybrook Institute.

Newkirk, Raymond L. (1989h). Revised Approach for the Design of the Software Development Human Activity System. San Francisco: Saybrook Institute.

Newkirk, Raymond L. (1989i). A Review of the Traditional Approach to Computer Software Development – An Ideology Critique. San Francisco: Saybrook Institute.

Newkirk, Raymond L. (1989j). The Creativity Myth: A New Software Design Paradigm for the 21st Century and Beyond. San Francisco: Saybrook Institute.

Newkirk, Raymond L. (1990a). SPAC Real Time Processing System Operational Evaluation Audit Handbook, Vol. I. Pleasant Hill, CA: Systems Management Institute Press.

Newkirk, Raymond L. (1990b). SPAC Real Time Processing System Operational Evaluation Audit Handbook, Vol.II. Pleasant Hill, CA: Systems Management Institute Press.

Newkirk, Raymond L. (1990c). Design Evaluation and Measurement: Evolutionary Guidance. System San Francisco: Saybrook Institute.

Newkirk, Raymond L. (1990d). Executive Information Systems: Foundation for Tomorrow. Pleasant Hill, CA: Systems Management Institute.

Newkirk, Raymond L. (1990e). The Design of the Software Development Group as a Systems Issue. San Francisco: Saybrook Institute.

Newkirk, Raymond L. (1990f). A Research Proposal for the Redesign of the Software Quality and Control Group. San Francisco: Saybrook Institute.

Newkirk, Raymond L. (1991a). Metamethodology Design Foundation for Tomorrow. Pleasant Hill, CA: Systems Management Institute.

Newkirk, Raymond L. (1991b). Philosophical Foundation of a Metamethodology for Design Inquiry in Software Development Human Activity Systems. San Francisco, CA: Saybrook.

Newkirk, Raymond L. (1992). Using the Human Systems Methodology to Design the Strategic Organization. Concord, CA: Systems Management Institute (Seminar Presentation).

Niebling, Carl & Christie, Marian (1991). Competitive Behavior. Wassenaar, The Netherlands: Niebling Productions.

NIST (2018). Cybersecurity is Everyone's Job. Publication of the National Initiative for Cybersecurity Education Working Group: Subgroup on Workforce Management at the National Institute of Standards and Technology.

Norman, Maxwell H. (1974). Dimensions of the Future Alternatives for Tomorrow. New York: Holt, Rinehart and Winston, Inc.

-O-

O'Connell, Patrick, F. St Francis of Assisi: The Spirituality of Conformation, Spirituality Today, Winder 1986, Vol. 38, pp. 1-11.

Offerman, Lynn R. & Growing, Marilyn K. (1990, February). Organizations of the Future: Changes and Challenges. American Psychologist, 45(2), pp. 95-108.

Ohmae, Kenichi (1990). The Borderless World: Power and Strategy in the Interlinked Economy. New York: Harper Business, Harper Collins Publishers.

Oldham, John M., M.D. & Morris, Lois B. (1990). Personality Self-Portrait: Why You Think, Work, Love, and Act the Way You Do. New York: Bantam Books.

Olle, Hagelstein, et al. (1988). Information Systems Methodologies: A Framework for Understanding. Menlo Park, CA: Addison-Wesley Publishing Company.

Ormerod, R.J (2008). The Transformation Competence Perspective. University of Warwick, Coventry, UK

Oskamp, Stuart (1990). Overconfidence in Case-Study Judgments. Judgment Under Uncertainty: Heuristics and Biases. Kahneman, Slovic & Tversky (Eds.), Cambridge, England: Cambridge University Press.

Ouellette, L. Paul (1992). How to Market the I/S Department Internally: Gaining the Recognition & Strategic Position You Merit. New York: AMACOM.

Overton, Willis F. (1975). General Systems, Structure, and Development. Structure and Transformation: Developmental and Historical Aspects, Volume 3., Chapter 4. John Wiley & Sons., Inc.

Overton, Willis F. & Ennis, Michelle D. (2006). Cognitive-Developmental and Behavioral-Analytic Theories: Evolving into Complementarity. Journal of Human Develoipment. Temple U.

-P-

Pagels, Heinz (1988). The Dreams of Reason: The Computer and the Rise of the Sciences of Complexity. New York: Simon and Schuster.

Pandikattu, Kuruvilla (2005). Spiritual Information for Integral Transformation, Spiritual Information 100 Perspectives on Science and Religion, Charles L. Harper, Jr. ed. Philadelphia, PA: Templeton Foundation Press.

Parberry, Ian (1987). Parallel Complexity Theory. New York: John Wiley & Sons.

Parikh, Girisj (1982). How to Measure Programmer Productivity. Wellesley, MA: Q.E.D. Information Sciences, Inc.

Parker, D. B. (1976). Crime by Computer. New York: Scribner's.

Parker, Nycum & Oura (1973). Computer Abuse. Washington, D. C: National Technical Information Service.

Pascale, Richard Tanner (1990). Managing on the Edge: How the Smartest Companies Use Conflict to Stay Ahead New York: Simon and Schuster.

Pasmore, William A. (1988). Designing Effective Organizations: The Sociotechnical Systems Perspective. New York: John Wiley & Sons.

Pava, C. (1983). Managing New Office Technology: An Organizational Strategy. New York: The Free Press.

Pelikan, Jaroslav, and Lehmann, Helmut T. eds. Luther's Works, 56 vols. St. Louis: Concordia Publishing House. Philadelphia: Fortress Press, 1955: 37:228.

Penzias, Arno (1989). IDEAS and Information. New York: Simon Schuster, Inc.

Perlmutter, H. (1965). Towards a Theory and Practice of Human Architecture. London: Tavistock.

Perls, Frederick S. (1971). Gestalt Therapy Verbatim. New York: Bantam Books.

Perry, D. E. & Kaiser, G. E. (1991, March). Models of Software Development Environments. IEEE Transactions on Software Engineering,17(3). College Park, MD: IEEE Computer Society.

Perry, William (1986). A Standard for Auditing Computer Applications: Selected Audit Areas Pennsauken, NJ: Auerbach Publishers, Inc.

Perry, William (1986). A Standard for Auditing Computer Applications: Auditing Microcomputer Systems. Pennsauken, NJ: Auerbach Publishers, Inc.

Perry, William (1986). Cleaning Up a Computer Mess: A Guide to Diagnosing and Correcting Computer Problems. New York: Van Nostrand Reinhold Company.

Perry, William (1987). A Standard for Testing Applications Software: Testing Computer Security. Boston: Auerbach Publishers, Inc.

Peters, Tom (1987). Thriving on Chaos: The Handbook for a Management Revolution. New York: Alfred A. Knopf.

Peters, Tom (1993). Liberation Management. New York: Random House.

Peters, Tom & Waterman, Robert H., Jr. (1982). In Search of Excellence. New York: Alfred A. Knopf.

Peters, Tom & Austin, Nancy (1983). A Passion for Excellence. New York: Alfred A. Knopf.

Peterson, Richard B. & Tracy, Lane (1979). Systematic Management of Human Resources Reading, MA: Addison-Wesley Publishing Company.

Petrie, H. G. (1968). The Strategy Sense of Methodology. Philosophy of Science, pp. 248-257.

Polinpapilinho, F. Katina & Ra'ed, M. Jaradat: A Three-Phase Framework for Elicitation of

Infrastructure Requirements. International Journal Critical Infrastructures. Vol. 8, Nos. 2/3, 2012. National Centers for System of Systems Engineering, Norfolk, VA 23508, USA

Polinpapilinho F. Katina and Charles B. Keating. Metasystem Pathologies: Towards Discovering of Impediments to System Performance. The National Centers for System of Systems Engineering Department of Engineering Management and Systems Engineering. Old Dominion University, Norfolk, VA Proceedings of the 2016 Industrial and Systems Engineering Research Conference. H. Yang, Z. Kong, and MD Sarder, eds.

Polkinghorne, Donald (1983). Methodology for the Human Sciences: Systems of Inquiry. Albany: State University of New York Press.

Pontifex, Mark & Illtyd, Trethowan (1953). Meaning of Existence. London: Longmans, Green and Company

Posner, Michael I. (ED.) (1989). Foundations of Cognitive Science. Cambridge, MA: MIT Press.

Pouvreau, David (2009). The Dialectical Tragedy of the Concept of Wholeness: Ludwig von Bertalanffy's Biography Revisited. Exploring Unity through Diversity: Volume 1

Pouvreau, David (2013). The Project of "General Systemology" Instigated by Ludwig Von Bertalanffy Genealogy, Genesis, Reception and Advancement. Bertalanffy Center for the Study of Systems Science, Vienna, Austria.

Pouvreau, David (2014). On the History of Ludwig Von Bertalanffy's "General Systemology", and on Its Relationship to Cybernetics - Part II: Contexts and Developments of the Systemological Hermeneutics Instigated by Von Bertalanffy. International Journal of General Systems.

Prevention Committee President's Council on Integrity and Efficiency (1986). Computer: Crimes, Clues and Controls. Washington, D. C: Prevention Committee President's Council on Integrity and Efficiency.

Prigogine, I. (1976). Order through Fluctuation: Self-Organization and Social Systems. Jantsch, E. & Waddington, C. H. (Eds.). Evolution and Consciousness: Human Systems in Transitions. Reading, MA: Addison-Wesley Publishing Company.

Prince, Howard T., II (1985). (Ed.), Leadership in Organizations. West Point: Associates, The Department of Behavioral Science and Leadership, United States Military Academy

Probity, Inc. (1990). Tools and Techniques of Basic Project Management. Tucson: Probity, Inc

Progoff, Ira (1990). Forward, in Mysticism: The Preeminent Study in the Nature and Development of Spiritual Consciousness. Twelfth Edition. Underhill, Evelyn (1990) New York, New York: Doubleday.

Pugh, D. S., Hickson, D. J., & Hinings, C. R. (1964). Writers on Structure of Functioning of Management of People in Organizations in Society. New York: Penguin Books.

-Q-

QED Information Sciences, Inc. (1985a). Security Evaluation for Small Computer Centers. Wellesley, MA: Q.E.D. Information Sciences, Inc.

QED Information Sciences, Inc. (1985b). Disaster Recovery: Contingency Planning and Program Evaluation. Wellesley, MA: Q.E.D. Information Sciences, Inc.

QED Information Sciences, Inc. (1985c). Personnel Productivity Management: Organization, Planning, Implementation and Control. Wellesley, MA: Q.E.D. Information Sciences, Inc.

Quick, James C. & Quick, Jonathan D. (1984). Organizational Stress and Preventive Management. New York: McGraw-Hill Book Company.

Quinn, James Brian (1992). Intelligent Enterprises. New York: The Free Press.

-R-

Radner, Daisie & Radner, Michael (1982). Science and Unreason. Belmont, CA: Wadsworth Publishing Company.

Rado, Sandor (1969). Adaptational Psychodynamics: Motivation and Control. New York: Science House.

Rahman, M.A. (1993). People's Self-Development: Perspectives on Participatory Action Research: A Journey through Expecrience. Zed Books: London.

Ramirez, Rafael, Ph.D. (1991). The Beauty of Social Organization. Munich: ACCEDO Verlagsgesellschaft mbH.

Ramamoorthy, C. V., et al. (1990). The Evolution Support Environment. IEEE Transactions on Software Engineering,16 (11), pp. 1225-1235.

Ray, Michael and Myers, Rochelle (1986). Creativity in Business. New York: Doubleday.

Reason, P. & Rowan, J. (1981). (Eds.) Human Inquiry: A Sourcebook of New Paradigm Research. Chichester, England: Wiley & Sons.

Reason, P. (ed.) (1988). Human Inquiry in Action: Developments in New Paradigm Research. Sage: London.

Reckmeyer, W. J. (1982). The Emerging Systems Paradigm: A Historical Perspective. Washington, D. C: The American University (Unpublished Doctoral Dissertation).

Ritzer, G. (1977). Working: Conflict and Change. Englewood Cliffs: Prentice-Hall, Inc.

Robertson, Scott P., et al. (1991). Human Factors in Computing Systems: Reaching through Technology, CHI'91 Conference Proceedings. Sponsored by the ACM's SIG on Computer Human Interaction. New York: The Association for Computing Machinery

Robinson, Peter (1991). Real-Time Processing System Presentation. Los Angeles: Security Pacific Automation Company.

Roeber, Richard J. C. (1973). The Organization in a Changing Environment. Reading, MA: Addison- Wesley Publishing Company.

Roethlisberger, F. & Dickson, J. J. (1939). Management and the Worker. Cambridge, MA: Harvard University Press.

Rogers, Joyce. Mysticism as a Way of Spirituality, Spirituality Today, Summer 1988, Vol. 40 No. 2, pp. 100-108.

Rolheiser, Ronald (1999). The Holy Longing: The Search for a Christian Spirituality. Doubleday, New York, New York.

Rorty, Richard (1981). Philosophy and the Mirror of Nature. Princeton, New Jersey: Princeton University Press.

Rorty, Richard (1998). Truth and Progress, Philosophical Papers, Volume 3. New York: Cambridge University Press.

Rosen, Robert H., Ph.D. (1991). The Healthy Company: Eight Strategies to Develop People, Productivity, and Profits. Los Angeles: Jeremy P. Tarcher, Inc.

Rosenau, Pauline Marie (1992). Post-Modernism and the Social Sciences: Insights, Inroads, and Intrusions. Princeton, NJ: Princeton University Press.

Rosenbaum, Stephanie (1989). The Role of Human Factors and Usability Testing in the Software Testing Process. Sixth International Conference on Testing Computer Software, May 25, 1989. Ann Arbor, MI: Tec-Ed Technical Publications and Graphics Services.

Rosenbluth, Hal F. & Peters, Diane McFerrin (1992). The Customer Comes Second and Other Secrets of Exceptional Service. New York: William Morrow and Company, Inc.

Roy, Sonam (2016). Insiders and Insider Threats an Overview of Definitions and Mitigation Techniques. Indian Institute of Space Science and Technology, Thiruvananthapu.

RTPS Operational Evaluation Team (1991). Real Time Processing System (RTPS) Operational Evaluation Analysis. Los Angeles: Security Pacific Automation Company.

RTPS Project Team (1989). Security Pacific Automation Company Real Time Processing System Project High-Level Requirements Document. Los Angeles: SPAC

RTPS Project Team (1990). Security Pacific Automation Company Real Time Processing Project Supplementary. Systems Management Institute, Pleasant Hill, CA.

Ruchlis, Hy & Oddo, Sandra (1990). Clear Thinking: A Practical Introduction. Buffalo: Prometheus Books.

Runes, Dagobert D. (1967). The Treasury of Philosophy. Totowa, NJ: Littlefield, Adams & Company.

Ruscoe, G.C., Fell, R.L., et al. (1985). The Application of Living Systems Theory to 41 U.S. Army Battalions. Behavioral Science, 30, pp. 7-52.

Russell, Jeffrey Burton (2005). Historical Errors Impeding Progress in Science and Religion, Spiritual Information 100 Perspectives on Science and Religion. Charles L. Harper, Jr. (Ed.). Philadelphia, PA: Templeton Foundation Press. pp. 63-67.

Russell, P. (1983). The Global Brain. Los Angeles: J. P. Tarcher.

Russo, J. Edward & Schoemaker, Paul J. H. (1989). Decision Traps: The Ten Barriers to Brilliant Decision-Making and How to Overcome Them. New York: Simon & Schuster, Inc.

-S-

Sackman, Harold (1971). Mass Information Utilities and Social Excellence. New York: Auerbach Publishers.

Sakaiya, Taichi (1991). The Knowledge-Value Revolution or a History of the Future. New York: Kodansha International

Salk, Jonas (1983). Autonomy of Reality: Merging of Intuition and Reason. New York: Columbia University Press.

Salner, Marcia (1985). The Relationship of Naive Epistemology to Formal Epistemology: Implications for the Teaching of Human Science Methodology, Methods, Donald E. Polkinghorne (Ed.). San Francisco: Saybrook.

Sampson, Edward E. (1983). Justice and the Critique of Pure Psychology. New York: Plenum Press.

Savary, Louis M., Berne, Patricia H., & Williams, Strephon Kaplan (1984). Dreams and Spiritual Growth: A Christian Approach to Dreamwork. Ramsey, N.J: Paulist Press.

Schank, Roger & Childers, Peter (1988). The Creative Attitude: Learning to Ask and Answer the Right Questions. New York: Macmillan Publishing Company.

Scharfstein, Ben-Ami, et al. (1978). Philosophy East Philosophy West: A Critical Comparison of Indian, Chinese, Islamic, and European Philosophy. Ben-Ami Scharfstein (Ed.). New York: Oxford University Press

Schloss, Jeffrey, (2005). Hath Darwin Suffered a Prophet's Scorn? Spiritual Information: 100 Perspectives on Science and Religion, Charles L. Harper, Jr. ed. Philadelphia, PA: Templeton Foundation Press, 2005.

Schneiders, Sandra, (2005). The Study of Christian Spirituality: Contours and Dynamics of a Discipline, Minding the Spirit: The Study of Christian Spirituality. Elizabeth A. Dreyer & Marki S. Burrows eds. Baltimore, MD: The Johns Hopkins University Press.

Schneiders, Sandra, (2005). A Hermeneutical Approach to the Study of Christian Spirituality, Minding the Spirit: The Study of Christian Spirituality. Elizabeth A. Dreyer & Marki S. Burrows eds. Baltimore, MD: The Johns Hopkins University Press.

Security Pacific Automation Company (1989a). ADS/Se Software Engineering Methodology. Los Angeles: Security Pacific Automation Company.

Security Pacific Automation Company (1989b). Real-Time Processing System Project High-Level Requirements Document. Los Angeles: Security Pacific Automation Company, RTPS Project Team.

Security Pacific Automation Company (1991). RTPS: Real Time Processing System Operational Evaluation Analysis. Los Angeles: Security Pacific Automation Company.

Semke, Jeannette & Nurius, Paula (1990, September). Information Structure, Information Technology and the Human Service Organizational Environment. Proceedings of the conference on computers and the Qualityof Life CQL '90. Washington, D.C., The George Washington University: ACM Special Interest Group on Computers & Society and ACM Special Interest Group on Computers and the Physically Handicapped, p. 20.

Senge, Peter M. (1990). The Fifth Discipline: The Art & Practice of the Learning Organization. New York: Doubleday.

Shaeffer, Francis (1990). Escape from Reason, in the Francis A. Shaeffer Triology. Westchester, IL: Crossway.

Sheldrake, Rupert (1981). A New Science of Life: The Hypothesis of Formative Causation. Los Angeles: Jeremy P. Tarcher, Inc.

Shick, Deana & Kyle O'Meara (2016). A Unique Approach to Threat Analysis Mapping: A Malware-Centric Methodology for Better Understanding, the Adversary Landscape.

Shneiderman, Ben (1991, January). Human Values and the Future of Technology: A Declaration of Responsibility. SIGCHI Bulletin, 23(1). New York: Association for Computing Machinery.

Silberstein, Michael (2005). On the Perennial Oneness of Being, Spiritual Information: 100 Perspectives on Science and Religion, Charles L. Harper, Jr. ed. Philadelphia, PA: Templeton Foundation Press, 2005.

Siler, Todd (1990). Breaking the Mind Barrier. New York: Simon & Schuster.

Silva, Michael & Sjogren, Bertil (1990). Europe 1992 & the New World Power Game. New York: John Wiley & Sons.

Silver, Susan (1989). Organized to Be the Best! Los Angeles: Adams-Hall Publishing.

Simon, Hebert A. (1964). The Architecture of Complexity. Readings in Managerial Psychology, Second Edition. Leavitt, Harold J. & Pondy, Louis R. (Eds.). Chicago: The University of Chicago Press.

Simon, Hebert A. (1969). The Sciences of the Artificial. Cambridge, MA: MIT Press.

Slawski, C. (1987). Causing Social Change. Proceedings of the Society for General Systems Research, Supplement, pp. 66-86.

Sloma, Richard S. (1977). No-Nonsense Management. New York: Bantam Books.

SMI (1990a). Systems Management Institute Audit Team Handbook for the RTPS Operational Evaluation and Performance Test Phase, Vol.1. Pleasant Hill, CA: Systems Management Institute Press.

SMI (1990a). Systems Management Institute Audit Team Handbook for the RTPS Operational Evaluation and Performance Test Phase, Vol. 2. Pleasant Hill, CA: Systems Management Institute Press.

SMI (1990a). Systems Management Institute Audit Team Handbook for the RTPS Operational Evaluation and Performance Test Phase, Vol. 3. Pleasant Hill, CA: SMI Press.

Smith, James K. A. (2006). Who's Afraid of Postmodernism Taking Derrida, Lyotard, and Foucault to Church. Grand Rapids, Michigan: Baker Academic.

Smolarski, Dennis C. (1988). The Spirituality of Computers, Spirituality Today, Winter 1988, Vol. 40 No. 4, pp. 292-307.

Sommer, R. (1974). Tight Spaces: Hard Architecture and How to Humanize It. Englewood Cliffs: Prentice-Hall, Inc

Spirn, J. R. (1977). Program Behavior: Models and Measurements. New York: Elsevier

Stamps, Jeffrey S. (1980). Holonomy: A Human Systems Theory. Seaside, CA: Intersystems.

Stanat, Ruth (1990). The Intelligent Corporation: Creating a Shared Network for Information and Profit. New York: American Management Association.

Stannard, F. Russell (2005). Proof or Persuasion? Spiritual Information: 100 Perspectves on Science and Religion, Charles L. Harper, Jr. ed. Philadelphia, PA: Templeton Foundation Press, 2005.

Steers, R. M. (1977). Organizational Effectiveness: A Behavioral View. Santa Monica, CA: Goodyear.

Stern, Nancy & Stern, Robert A. (1983). Computers in Society. Englewood Cliffs: Prentice-Hall.

Sternberg, Robert J. (1988). The Triarchic Mind: A New Theory of Human Intelligence. New York: Penguin Books.

Stewart, Hugh B. (1989). Recollecting the Future: A View of Business, Technology, and Innovation in the Next 30 Years. Homewood, IL: Dow Jones-Irwin.

Stich, Stephen P. (Ed.) (1975). Innate Ideas. Berkeley, CA: University of California Press

Strauss, Danie (2016). The Tension between (Methodological) Individualism and Holism. Journal of Christian Scholarship.

Studenmund, A. H. (2013). Using Econometrics, Pearson

Suarez, Antoine (2005). Do Quantum Experiments Challenge Kant's Criticism of the Proofs for the Existence of God? Spiritual Information: 100 Perspectves on Science and Religion, Charles L. Harper, Jr. ed. Philadelphia, PA: Templeton Foundation Press, 2005.

Suarez, Francis (1947). On the Various Kinds of Distinctions. Translated by Cyril Vollert in the: Disputationes Metaphysicae, Disp. No. 7. Milwaukee, WI: Marquette University Press

Sutherland, J. W. (1973). A General Systems Philosophy for the Social and Behavioral Sciences. New York: George Braziller.

-T-

Taket, Ann & White, Leroy (1996). Pragmatic Pluralism, an Explication. Systems Practice, 9(6), 571-586.

Talbot, Michael (1991). The Holographic Universe. New York: Harper Collins Publishers.

Tapscott, Don & Caston, Art (1993). Paradigm Shift the New Promise of Information Technology. New York: McGraw Hill, Inc.

Taylor, Charles (1989). Sources of the Self: The Making of the Modern Identity. Cambridge, MA: Harvard University Press.

Teilhard de Chardin, Pierre (1965). The Phenomenon of Man (2nd ed.). New Your York.

Terninko, John (2011): 40 Inventive Principles with Social Examples. Responsible Management 62 Case Rd. Nottingham, NH 03290-5507 USA

Thayer, Frederick (1972). General System(s) Theory: The Promise That Could Not Be Kept, Academy of Management Journal, XV (1972).

Thomas, Keith A. (1987). Building an Open System. New York: Van Nostrand Reinhold Company.

Thompson, James D. (1976). Organizations in Action. New York: McGraw-Hill Book Company.

Thompson, John B. (1984). Studies in the Theory of Ideology. Berkeley, CA: University of California Press.

Thomsett, Rob (1993). Third Wave Project Management: A Handbook for Managing the Complex Information Systems for the 1990s. Englewood Cliffs: Prentice Hall, Inc.

Tinbergen, Jan (1958). The Design of Development. The International Development Institute,

International Bank for Reconstruction and Development. Baltimore, MD: The Johns Hopkins Press.

Todd, Mary Anne & Guitian, Constance (1989). Computer Security Training Guidelines. Washington, D.C: National Institute of Standards and Technology.

Toffler, A. (1971). Future Shock. New York: Bantam Books.

Toffler, A. (1980). The Third Wave. New York: Bantam Books.

Toffler, A. (1990). Power Shift: Knowledge, Wealth, and Violence at the Edge of the 21st Century. New York: Bantam Books.

Tosi, Henry L. & Hammer, W. Clay (Eds.) (1977). Organizational Behavior and Management: A Contingency Approach. Chicago: St. Clair Press.

Trist, E.L. (1978). Adapting to a Changing World. Readings in Quality of Working Life, George F. Sanderson, (Ed.). Ottawa: Labour Canada, pp. 10-20

Tschudin, Alain J-P. C. (2005). Preparing the Way for the lord: Evolution, Christianity, and the Dialog on Moral Freedom, Spiritual Information: 100 Perspectves on Science and Religion, Charles L. Harper, Jr. ed. Philadelphia, PA: Templeton Foundation Press, 2005.

Tsoukas, Haridimos; Papoulias, Demetrios B. (1996). Creativity in OR/MS: From Technique to Epistemology: Interfaces, 26(2), 73-79.

Turnage, Janet J. (1990, February). The Challenge of New Workplace Technology for Psychology. American Psychologist, 45(2), pp. 171-178.

-U-

Ulrich, Werner (1983). Critical Heuristics of Social Planing: A New Approach to Practical Philosophy. Wiley: Chichester.

Underhill, Evelyn (1990). Mysticism: The Preeminent Study in the Nature and Development of Spiritual Consciousness. Twelfth Edition. New York, New York: Doubleday.

-V-

Van Fleet, James K. (1983). 25 Steps to Power and Mastery over People. West Nyack, NY: Parker Publishing Company, Inc

Vam Kaam, Adrian, Fr. & Muto, Susan, Dr. (1978). Questions and Answers on Formative Spirituality: Am I Living a Spiritual Life? Dimension Books, New Jersey.

Vetter, Jennifer, (Ed.). (2016). Franciscan Virtues through the Year: 52 Steps to Conversion from St. Francis of Assisi. Written by Members of the Confraternity of Penitents.

Vost, Kevin (2018). How to Think Like Aquinas. Sophia Institute Press: Manchester, New Hampshire.

-W-

Wack, John P. & Carnahan, Lisa A. (1989). Computer Viruses and Related Threat s: A Management Guide. Washington, D. C: National Institute of Standards and Technology.

Wadsworth (1973). The Human Side of Data Processing Management. Englewood Cliffs: Prentice-Hall, Inc.

Wagner, Clare (1985). Current Trends: Spirituality in a Dark Age: Some Reflections," Spirituality Today, Spring 1985, Vol. 37, pp. 59-71.

Wallace, Robert H., Stockenberg, John E., & Charette, Robert N. (1987). A Unified Methodology for Developing Systems. New York: Intertext Publications, Inc., McGraw-Hill, Inc.

Walsh, Mike (1991). Productivity Sand Traps & Tar Pits: How to Detect and Avoid Them. New York: Dorset House Publishing.

Walsh, Myles E. (1981). Understanding Computers: What Managers and Users Need to Know. New York: John Wiley & Sons.

Walshe, T. J. (1933). Quest of Reality. Saint Louis, MO: B. Herder Book Company.

Warfield, J. N. (1987a). Education in Generic Design. Bela Banathy (Ed.). Design inquiry, pp. 185-196. San Francisco: International Systems Institute & International Society for General Systems Research.

Warshaw, Leon J. (1979). Managing Stress. Reading, MA: Addison-Wesley Publishing Company.

Watkins, J. W. N. (1953). Ideal Types and Historical Explanation, in H. Feigl & M. Brodbeck (EDs.), Readings in the Philosophy of Science. New York.

Watkins, J. W. N. (1958). The Alleged Inadequacy of Methodological Individualism, Journal of Philosophy, LV (1958).

Watkins, J. W. N. (1959). Historical Explanation in the Social Sciences, in Patrick Gardiner (Ed.), Theories of History. New York.

Watson, Paul K. (2005). Living Purpose: The Study of Purpose in the Living World as a Sources of New Spiritual Information, Spiritual Information 100 Perspectives on Science and Religion, Charles L. Harper, Jr. (Ed.). Philadelphia, PA: Templeton Foundation Press. (p. 301).

Weber, Zach: Paradox and Foundation. Submitted in Total Fulfillment of the Requirements of the Degree of Doctor of Philosophy.May 2009

Weinberg, Gerald M. (1975). An Introduction to General Systems Thinking. New York: John Wiley & Sons.

Weinberg, Gerald M. (1982). Overstructured Management of Software Engineering. Proceedings, Sixth International Conference of Software Engineering. Washington, D.C: IEEE Computer Society. Pp.2-8.

Weinberg, Gerald M. (1986). Becoming a Technical Leader: An Organic Problem-Solving Approach. New York: Dorset House Publishing Company.

Weinberg, Gerald M. (1992). Quality Software Management Volume 1 Systems Thinking. New York: Dorset House Publishing.

Weinberg, Harry L. (1959) Levels of Knowing and Existence. Harper & Brothers, Publishers New York.

Weisbord, Marvin R. (1987). Productive Workplaces: Organizing and Managing for Dignity, Meaning, and Community. San Francisco: Jossey-Bass Publishers

Weiss, Paul (1967). The Living System: Determinism Stratified, in Koestler & Smythies, Beyond Reductionism. New York.

Weiss, Paul (1967). One Plus One Does Not Equal Two, in G. C. Quarton, T. Melnechuk, & F. O. Schmitt (EDs.), The Neurosciences: A Study Program. New York.

Wexley & Yukl (1977). Organizational Behavior and Personnel Psychology. Homewood, IL: Richard D. Irwin, Inc.

Wheatley, Edward W. (1976). Values in Conflict. Miami: Banyan Books.

Wheelwright, Steven C. & Makridakis, Spyros (1980). Forecasting Methods for Management, 3rd Ed. New York: John Wiley & Sons.

Whitaker, Randall, Essler, Ulf & Ostberg, Olov (1991). Participatory Business Modeling. Sweden: Lulea University, Research Report, Tulea 1991: 31.

Whitehead, Alfred N. (1929). Process and Reality. New York: The Free Press.

Whyte, W.F. (ed.) (1991) Participatory Action Research. Sage: London.

Wilber, Ken (2000). Integral Psychology: Consciousness, Spirit, Psychology, Therapy. Shambhala Publications House, Boston, MA.

Wildman, Wesley J. (2005). Global Spiritual Confusion and the Neglected Problem of Excess Spiritual Information, Spiritual Information 100 Perspectives on Science and Religion, Charles L. Harper, Jr. (Ed.). Philadelphia, PA: Templeton Foundation Press. (pp. 33-38).

Williams, Raymond (1989). The Politics of Moderism. New York: Verso.

Wilson, Anne. Holistic Spirituality, Spirituality Today, Autumn 1988, Vol. 40 No. 3, pp. 208-219.

Wiseman, James A. Teachning Spiritual Theology: Methodological Reflections, Spirituality Today, Summer 1989, Vol. 41 No. 2, pp. 143-159.

Wittgenstein, L. (1961). Tractatus Logico-Philosophicus. London: Routledge & Kegan Paul.

Wolman, Benjamin D. (Ed.). (1973). Handbook of General Psychology. Englewood Cliffs: Prentice-Hall, Inc.

Wood, C. C., et al. (1987). Computer Security: A Comprehensive Controls Checklist. New York: John Wiley & Sons.

Woodcock, Alexander & Davis, Monte (1978). Catastrophe Theory. New York: Penguin Theory.

Woodson, Wesley E. (1987). Human Factors Reference Guide for Electronics and Computer Professionals. New York: McGraw-Hill Book Company.

Wooldridge, Susan, Corder, Colin, & Johnson, Calude (1973). Security Standards for Data Processing. New York: John Wiley $ Sons.

Wriston, Walter B. (1992). The Twilight of Sovereignty: How the Information Revolution is Transforming Our World. New York: Charles Scribner's Son's.

-Y-

Yolles M. I. (1996): Critical Systems Thinking, Paradigms, and the Modelling Space. Systems Practice,

Yourdon, Edward (1992). Decline & Fall of the American Programmer. Englewood Cliffs: Yourdon Press.

-Z-

Zandar, Alvin (1994). Making Groups Effective, 2nd Edition. Jossey Bass Publishers, San Francisco.

Zedeck, Sheldon & Mosier, Kethleen (1990, February). Work in the Family and Employing Organization, American Psychologist. 45(2), pp. 24-251.

Zerzan, John & Carnes, Alice (1988). Questioning Technology. London: Freedom Press.

Zuboff, Shoshana (1984). In the Age of the Smart Machine: The Future of Work and Power. New York: Basic Books.

Zuker, Elaina (1991). The Seven Secrets of Influence. New York: McGraw-Hill, Inc.

Zvegintzov, N. (1982). What Life? What Cycle? Proceedings of the National Computer Conference. Reston, VA: AFIPS Press, pp. 563-568.

Zwart, Martin (1990). Constraint Driven Design/Engineering. Amsterdam: P.Q.Information Group, b.v., Mosselaan 57, 1934 PJ, Egmond a/d Hoef Netherlands.

Zwart, Martin (1991a). Integration of Workflow & EXTRA. Amsterdam: P.Q. Information Group, b. v.

Zwart, Martin (1991b). Object Documentation System. Amsterdam: P.Q. Information Group.

About the Author

Dr. Raymond Leslie Newkirk, Psy.D., Ph.D., Ph.D., C.Q.A., F.B.I.M., I.O.M.

Founder, Entrepreneur, Product Architect, Inventive Problem Solver, Virtual-Learning Pioneer, Deep Technology Scientist, Thought Leader, Podcaster, Consultant, Mentor, Publisher Author, Speaker, Internationally Ranked Athlete

Raymond L. Newkirk is an internationally respected consulting specialist having earned advanced degrees and certifications in several disciplines including Ph.Ds. in the Philosophy of Science and Behavioral Science, Psy.D. in Clinical Psychology, Th.C., in Theology and the Ph.D. with Distinction in Human Science. Dr. Newkirk originated the Ulthule™ approach to human performance and the Applied Intuitive Solutions™ Inventive Problem-Solving Knowledge Base System. His professional background includes a distinguished career in multicultural research, human system design, and executive development. He has presented the Keynote Address to global audiences. He is the Founder & CEO of the Systems Management Institute, a firm that applies human systems design to the building of high-performance organizations. He was Founder and Chairman of Bay University, an innovative E-Learning Company. He has enjoyed a life-long interest in business and enterprise incubation. He founded his first company at the age of 16, a janitorial service with three employees, and has organized start-ups & joint ventures ever since.

Dr. Newkirk has served in diverse industries and executive capacities. He was a Senior Fellow of the Monterey Bay Management Group. He served as Chief Operating Officer of Mindmaker, Inc. of San Jose, California, an early A/I and neural net pioneer that won Best of Comdex two years consecutively during the dot.com revolution in Silicon Valley. He also served as President and Chief Operating Officer of P.Q. Information Group, b.v. the Netherlands, an innovative company that pioneered Business Rules processing software development, and Founder of the International Association of Information Management.

He led projects for the Minister of Defense and Aviation and the Royal Saudi Naval Forces for the Kingdom of Saudi Arabia and for the Office of the President, Republic of the Philippines. Dr. Newkirk has led industry-changing engagements for Southwest Bell, Bank of America, and Dell Computers. He was a VIP Priority Guest of the CNN World Business Development Congress. He was invited as a visiting Ambassador in Business Development and Technology Transfer to the Soviet Union and as an expert guest to development conferences in Cairo, Egypt and Oxford, England. He conducted seminars for Technology Transfer, Rome, I.B.C. London and Amsterdam and S.I.B.C. Jeddah, Kingdom of Saudi Arabia.

Dr. Newkirk never stops writing. A prolific writer, he has published more than 1,600 articles, monographs, books, e-learning courses, blogs, and guest columns for the San Francisco Examiner. His latest book, Navigating Sociopaths at Work, will be available early in 2020. His most recent book, Leading by Design, has become a widely sought collector's book that is available through the Systems Management Institute Press, Amazon, or Booklocker Press. His next book series, Ray Newkirk Tackles Workplace Relationships, advances a fresh look at leadership thinking and establishes the foundation for a new science of Leadership. He has authored works in English, Italian, Russian, Arabic, and Latin.

He is the producer of the Ray Newkirk Library Series. He advocates the intellectual, physical, and spiritual development of the person. He studied philosophy as a Benedictine Monk in Italy and studied theology with the Franciscan Friars in Washington D.C. He participated for many years with the Amateur Athletic Union (AAU) both as a competitor and supporter. Early in his athletic career, he attained international ranking in Olympic Weightlifting having won 12 championships and set 22 competitive records in the sport. He won Outstanding Weightlifter Award, Ohio State A.A.U. A few of his many records still stand today. Currently, he is in training to compete in the Masters World Championships and was the reigning Pacific Weightlifting Association Masters Champion where he is still in the business of chasing records.

As an amateur explorer, Ray went diving in the Red Sea, mountain climbing in Alaska, worked as a deck hand on Dutch freighter, sailed in the Bahamas, and enjoyed deep-sea fishing in the Caribbean, among other global adventures. Dr. Newkirk is an innovative social thinker. He is concerned about the problems facing the elderly in this technological and fast paced age. He has conducted workshops for senior citizens & executives on health, nutrition, and stress management. He established a health clinic and medical network for the elderly. He also contributed to the establishment of an orphanage in the Third World, funded fellowships for students in Eastern Europe to travel abroad and participate in seminars and professional training, and established a Southeast Asian International Fellowship. Dr. Newkirk's Guiding Perspective is:

Life, Love, Leadership, Growth, & Honor

"Live life fully. Love deeply with wisdom.
Lead others to great achievement.
Grow spiritually and intellectually.
Honor God in all I do."

Agony, If Nothing Else, Is Life's Faithful Retribution for Entering an Ill-Advised Workplace Relationship

Don't miss out!

Visit the website below and you can sign up to receive emails whenever Dr. Raymond Leslie Newkirk publishes a new book. There's no charge and no obligation.

https://books2read.com/r/B-A-HJRKE-SFHLB

Did you love *The Psychology of Insider Threat Prevention Part 2*? Then you should read *Adventures in Paleo Leadership*[1] by Raymond Newkirk, Psy.D., Ph.D., Ph.D.!

[2]

Leadership is a vital topic in every profession from. Business, Education, Government. and Defense to Religion, Science, Medicine, and Law Enforcement, and on and on and on. Leadership often makes the difference between success and failure. It is one of those topics that fuels the emotions of just about everyone from age ten to one hundred. Everyone seems to have an opinion about Leadership. These opinions frequently contradict one another as they generate confusion among followers. I wrote "Adventures in Paleo Leadership" to take us back, way way back, to that time when Leadership first began to emerge in recorded human affairs and follow its evolutionary unfolding to better understand what Leadership is and how it became so confusing and complicated as it has become over the last several decades. From

1. https://books2read.com/u/mekZal

2. https://books2read.com/u/mekZal

Mysticism to Psychology and all topics in between, Leadership has been part to the human landscape since human beings first started being together. ----Raymond L. Newkirk

Also by Dr. Raymond Leslie Newkirk

21st Century Executive Life
21st Century Executive Life

Cosmic Truth God, Us and Them
Cosmic Truth: God, Us, and Them

Paleo-Leadership
Reconstructed Leadership
UlThule™ Leadership
Paleo Leadership Part 4

Systems Thinking in Requirements Analysis
Systems Thinking in Requirements Analysis

The Psychology of Insider Threat Prevention
The Psychology of Insider Threat Prevention Part 2
Psychology of Insider Threat Prevention Part 4
Insider Threat Prevention Part 5

Standalone

A Person Passing By

Sociopaths at Work

From Confusion to Clarity

www.ingramcontent.com/pod-product-compliance
Lightning Source LLC
LaVergne TN
LVHW022044200926
848481LV00003B/787